MW00784643

New Zealand's
Top Trout Fishing
Waters

New Zealand's Top Trout Fishing Waters

John Kent
Patti Magnano Madsen

REED

Published by Reed Books, a division of Reed Publishing (NZ) Ltd,
39 Rawene Rd, Birkenhead, Auckland.
Associated companies, branches and representatives throughout the world.

ISBN 0 7900 0877 7

Designed by Graeme Leather

First published 1997
This edition first published 2003

Printed in New Zealand

CONTENTS

LIST OF MAPS

FOREWORD

> So long as water moves, so long as fins press against it, so long as weather changes and man is fallible, fish will remain in some measure unpredictable. And so long as there is unpredictability, there will be luck, both good and bad.
>
> Roderick Haig-Brown
> *Measure of the Year*

Allow me to add: So long as there is unpredictability, there will be – adventure! With its thousands of miles of clear, free-flowing and undammed rivers; with its hundreds of pristine lakes; with its wild unplanted trout; with its extremely challenging fishing situations; with its tiny population and lack of industry; with one of the safest and loveliest settings on this planet, New Zealand is home to our finest fishing adventures.

There are always those zealots who guard their fishing destinations with a vengeance, who believe that 'others' equate to too many people in their fishing hole, who believe our sport suffers from too many new anglers and who would happily do away with all education and fishing references. I must confess that there are times in my fishing clinics when the thought of directing certain students to something else, like billiards or bowling, is most appealing. Fortunately that is not true of Patti and John, the authors of this excellent reference.

It is unlikely that any angler has explored all of the fishing possibilities that exist in this South Pacific paradise – but these two highly dedicated fly fishers have come a lot closer than most and are doing their damnedest to fish them all. They are very social and willing to share most of their discoveries, knowing that only in numbers and unity can we conserve our waters and that solitude is but a short walk away on most waters. You are lucky indeed to have found this work. I hope it will lead you to your own fishing adventure, perhaps even a fishing fairytale.

Mel Krieger

INTRODUCTION

There are over 700 rivers and 200 lakes in New Zealand worth fishing. New Zealand is a fly angler's paradise, as most rivers and lakes have excellent water quality and offer sight fishing to large wild brown and rainbow trout. There is virtually no private water and the licence fees are reasonable. Access to most rivers and lakes is easy and there are wilderness areas providing trophy trout for the adventurous. Many overseas anglers visiting New Zealand have limited time to fish and the wide range of water available can be confusing and overwhelming.

This book has been written to make that choice easier and to offer tips on fishing New Zealand waters. We have carefully selected our top spots but understand there are many others equally as good. To simplify the angler's itinerary we have endeavoured to group these fishing spots in close proximity to a central location so you have a choice of rivers and lakes to visit within a reasonable distance. We have also included information on the local fishing guides and tackle shops in the vicinity. And, to be well entertained on non-fishing days, various local attractions have been mentioned.

It has been our pleasure to have fished the top spots described and we hope this guide book will direct you to what we consider to be an angler's El Dorado and that you will share in our delight.

PLANNING

A trip to New Zealand

General

New Zealand's three main islands lie in the South Pacific between latitudes 34 and 47 degrees S. The highest point is Mt Cook at 3754 m. New Zealand is a long, narrow country – 1600 km long and 400 km across at the widest point. The total land area is similar to the state of Montana in the United States. Polynesian voyagers first populated New Zealand about 900 years ago and European colonisation began early in the nineteenth century.

Three quarters of the population of 3.8 million live in the North Island. Fourteen percent of these are Maori, living mostly in the North Island. There is also a significant Pacific Island and Asian population residing mainly in the largest city, Auckland. English is the common language.

Climate

New Zealand has a mild oceanic climate. A mixture of anticyclones and depressions, modified by the topography, produces a variable weather pattern which is often difficult to forecast. Much of the country receives over 2000 hours of sunshine per year. The prevailing westerly winds shed most of their moisture on the western side of both islands, leading to wide differences in rainfall. Parts of the west coast of the South Island receive up to 6000 mm of rain annually, with 8000 mm in the Southern Alps. On the eastern side of the Alps, in areas of Central Otago, rainfall can be as low as 300 mm per year. Significant characteristics of each district's climate will be detailed in the text.

Passport and visa

Visitors to New Zealand must carry a current passport, and a visa is required for stays of longer than three months. The maximum stay permitted for visitors is six months, or nine months in every 18-month period.

Customs regulations on entry

Because New Zealand is an agricultural country and is free of many exotic diseases such as foot and mouth, there are very strict biosecurity regulations. The Ministry of Agriculture and Forestry (MAF) quarantine service requires all incoming items of plant or animal origin to be declared, and exacts heavy penalties (including on-the-spot fines) for offenders. Commercially tied flies are normally acceptable but anything that has recently been in contact with foreign soil may be impounded for fumigation unless it has been scrupulously cleaned. Anglers are strongly advised to thoroughly clean and disinfect waders and boots before arrival. If fumigation is required, items may be held for about a week. If in any doubt we recommend that you check MAF's website at www.maf.govt.nz.

Banking and money

The currency is New Zealand dollars and cents. Banks, money exchanges and automatic teller machines (ATMs) are available in all cities and many towns. Credit cards are accepted in most places and full legal and commercial services are easily accessible.

A goods and services tax (GST) of 12.5 percent is included in the price of retail items unless stated otherwise. This tax also applies to services such as professional guiding.

Health system

Excellent medical and dental services are available; however, travellers are strongly advised to take out travel insurance before departure.

Cities

Auckland, in the north of the North Island, is by far the largest city, with a population of over one million. Wellington, at the southern end of the North Island, is the capital city and houses a democratically elected government. Christchurch and Dunedin are the main cities in the South Island, and Queenstown, in the southwest of the South Island, is a major tourist attraction and each city has its own special characteristics. Smaller cities and country towns also provide plenty of opportunities and facilities for the tourist angler.

☐ AUCKLAND

Auckland lies on a narrow isthmus between the Waitemata and Manukau harbours. The main street, Queen Street, leads to the waterfront and the Viaduct Basin, at present the base for America's Cup yachting. From here, ferries and pleasure craft offer access to the Hauraki Gulf Maritime Park and its many beautiful islands. This vibrant city has many restaurants, art galleries and shopping malls, as well as parks and gardens to explore. The city is dotted with extinct volcanic cones that provide easy landmarks by which visitors can orientate.

If you are spending a few days in Auckland, we suggest visiting Kelly Tarlton's Underwater World, the Auckland Museum, the Auckland Art Gallery and the Skytower. If the weather is favourable, take a cruise on the harbour and the Hauraki Gulf, or cross the Harbour Bridge to the North Shore, where there are safe beaches for swimming. There are excellent wineries near Henderson and on Waiheke Island.

For more information, contact the Auckland Visitor Centre at 287 Queen Street.

☐ CHRISTCHURCH

Christchurch is the South Island's largest city and has been described as 'the most English city outside England'. It is also known as the Garden City, and a walk through the Botanical Gardens and Hagley Park or along the banks of the Avon River is a must. There are outstanding cafés and restaurants and good shopping. The Antarctic Centre at the airport is well worth visiting and a ride on the gondola to the top of the Port Hills provides panoramic views of the city, Lyttelton Harbour, the Canterbury Plains and the Southern Alps. Take the tram to the Arts Centre located in the elegant stone Gothic Revival buildings, where there are theatres, craft studios, cafés and shops. Across Rolleston Avenue from the Arts Centre is the Canterbury Museum and across Montreal Street from the Arts Centre is the Christchurch Art Gallery. More information can be obtained from the Visitor Centre in Cathedral Square.

Transport

Internal air links to other centres are easy and reliable but can be expensive. Bus service is reasonable, but passenger rail services are available only between the main cities. Rental campervans and cars should be booked well before the summer holiday season (mid December to mid February). Rental agencies provide maps and do not generally charge drop-off fees. Driving is on the left-hand side of the road and vehicles are right-hand drive. Most roads are two-lane (one in each direction) and unsealed gravel roads are common in the countryside. Drivers who are not used to these conditions need to be extremely cautious as it is easy to lose control when cornering or travelling fast.

Visitors from other countries who carry a full driver's licence will not require an international driver's licence for the first 12 months from date of entry into New Zealand.

Interisland ferry services provide passenger and vehicular transport between the North and South Islands. It is important to book at least two months before the peak holiday season. The crossing takes up to three and a half hours and is very scenic.

The Automobile Association (AA) does not recommend buying a vehicle and selling it at the end of the trip unless you plan an extended holiday of two to three months. 'Buyer beware' is their advice.

Maps

Road maps can be purchased from the AA, bookshops and some service stations (garages). They may also be provided by camper-van and rental car operators. More detailed maps (1:50,000) can be bought from specialised map shops in the main centres, from Department of Conservation (DoC) offices or from the Information Map Centre, Private Bag 903, Upper Hutt, Wellington.

Accommodation

There is a wide range of accommodation available in New Zealand, but few luxury first-class hotels outside the main cities. Camping grounds, cabins, backpacker hostels, homestays, bed and breakfasts, farmstays, motels (most with cooking and laundry facilities), lodges and hotels offer an extensive selection and diverse experience.

Food

Grocery shopping is best done at urban supermarkets, where a wide selection is available. Dairies (convenience stores) and service stations supply a limited selection of groceries. They charge higher prices, but are open for longer hours. There are good cafés and restaurants in most towns. Prices tend to be high, but tipping is not the usual custom. Most menus are a la carte. Tap water is generally safe to drink unless clearly marked otherwise, but it is best to filter or boil water from streams and rivers.

Shopping

Information relating to tackle shops is detailed under each district. The main city centres generally have the best selection, but in provincial areas you are more likely to get advice on local conditions. For non-fishing days there are craft shops, art galleries, and antique stores to visit, often tucked away in the smallest of towns.

Electricity

New Zealand's power supply is 230 volts AC. Most hotels and motels provide 110-volt AC sockets for razors only, and an adapter or converter may be required as power outlets accept only flat two- or three-pin plugs.

Public holidays

Many facilities close on public holidays, although most shops are open on all except Christmas Day and Anzac Day. Public holidays include:

Christmas Day: 25 December
Boxing Day: 26 December
New Year: 1 and 2 January
Waitangi (New Zealand) Day: 6 February
Easter (includes Good Friday and Easter Monday)
Anzac Day: 25 April
Queen's Birthday: first Monday in June
Labour Day: third Monday in October

There are also one-day provincial holidays and school holidays at various times, from mid December to early February.

Telephone services

Most public phones use a phone card, which can be purchased from postal outlets, bookstores, dairies and service stations. Telecom accepts credit card payment for operator-assisted national and international calls. To dial overseas from New Zealand, first dial 00, then the country code (eg, 1 for the US), the area code and finally the local number. Consult the telephone directory for other calling information.

Cellphone coverage extends over most of New Zealand, but there are gaps, often in the remote places frequented by anglers.

☐ **Important phone numbers**

For all emergencies: 111
Local operator: 010
International operator: 0170
International directory: 0172

Time differences and daylight saving

New Zealand is 12 hours ahead of GMT (Greenwich Mean Time).

Standard time differences for the US are: Eastern – 17 hours behind New Zealand; Central – 18 hours behind; Mountain – 19 hours behind.

Daylight saving comes into effect on the first Sunday in October (clocks are advanced by one hour) and ends on the third Sunday in March.

UNIQUE FEATURES of New Zealand fishing

New Zealand fishing is magical, seductive, challenging and more captivating than fishing in the United States for a variety of reasons. It requires special skills and a thoughtful approach. Local weather patterns must be checked daily or well laid fishing plans could prove futile. Flexibility and local knowledge are of utmost importance. River and stream selection may need altering on the day because of wind or weather conditions. First-time anglers would be well advised to contact and hire professional guides local to each region.

A prerequisite for successfully fishing New Zealand waters is a good solid command of casting skills and a rod that meets the demands of windy conditions, longer tippets, weighted nymphs and streamside vegetation. Early season results are often measured by the weight of nymphs one can comfortably cast. To consistently make an accurate first cast is vital for good results. A well known New Zealand guide has stated there is an 80 percent chance of hooking a sighted fish on the first cast but the odds drop to 20 percent by the fourth. In addition, optimum water temperatures on average tend to be much cooler than, for example, those in the United States – on occasion, we have found fish rising to a dry in water at 11 degrees C (52 degrees F).

Tippets are heavier than those used by most anglers in, for example, the United States, but limp enough for a good drift. As well, the tippet must be stiff enough to turn over in windy conditions and strong enough to handle good-sized trout with some authority.

The water clarity in New Zealand can be exceptional and because the trout population is not high in most waters, spotting and stalking fish is the preferred technique on many rivers and lakes. This can be difficult to master and the use of a professional guide to help with this aspect of fishing is invaluable, especially for the first-time visiting angler. Good polarised sunglasses and the ability to 'read the water' are essential. Blind casting spooks more fish than one realises. As there may be only one fish in a run or pool, spotting that fish before casting is critical.

Even though heavily fished rivers present 'educated' trout that are difficult to seduce even with the smallest morsel, wilderness rivers rarely visited by an angler can be equally difficult. The slightest variation in normal surroundings, such as line shadow, jerky movements, wading bow-waves and body scent create enough disturbance to make the trout wary. There are exceptions to spotting and stalking – these include winter fishing in Rotorua and Taupo districts, float-tube or boat fishing, stream-mouth and night fishing.

Clothing that blends with the environment, keeping a low profile, and a stealthy approach enable the angler to move closer to a fish, thereby improving the accuracy of the cast. Use stream-side vegetation as camouflage and remember that trout have more difficulty seeing you when the sun is behind you. If there is glare on the water try crossing to the other side and make use of trees and scrub to minimise light reflection. Camouflage clothing is not necessary – dull brown, fawn, blue or green clothing is satisfactory. Avoid red, white and yellow.

For river fishing, wet-wading in boots and shorts is recommended, as there is usually a lot of walking involved. Heavy neoprene waders are fine for lake, stream mouth, winter or night fishing but become hot and cumbersome for back-country rivers. Lightweight waders can be damaged by thorny vegetation. Felt soles are very useful when wading some rivers, but can be dangerously slippery on steep grassy hillsides.

Whereas the best hatches in the United States occur on calm, misty and cloudy days, calm sunny days are best in New Zealand. Spotting fish takes precedence over hatch blizzards. The ultra-violet light intensity is high so protection creams and lip salve are essential, as is insect repellent, as sandflies and mosquitoes are very bothersome in some places.

To successfully fish most New Zealand rivers in summer, fitness and endurance are important. Good access to back-country streams can be limited and long days of tramping and walking rivers are often necessary. Being physically fit makes fishing in New Zealand much more enjoyable.

There are no harmful animals or predators in New Zealand and camping in the bush is safe. The biggest danger is the changeable weather: four seasons can be experienced in one fishing day so it is wise to carry extra clothing and a waterproof jacket.

In New Zealand very little fly fishing is done from boats or float-tubes, although both can be useful at times. The extra weight and baggage handling is not worth the effort, however.

Access to rivers and lakes is usually easy. The 'Queen's chain', a strip of public land, exists on most waterways. Effectively this means you can walk on riverbanks and lake frontages, provided there is public access to them in the first place. If there is no public access to waterways, permission must be obtained from the landowner (see 'Etiquette' below).

Conservation

New Zealand anglers are privileged to have some of the highest quality fishing for wild trout anywhere in the world. However, there is no room for complacency: the fishery must be protected.

In recent years, fish and game councils have sensibly reduced the bag limit in most districts, and most New Zealand anglers are now practising catch and release and other conservation measures.

➢ Use the strongest practical nylon tippets to facilitate quick landing of fish. Long playing leads to the build-up of harmful metabolites such as lactic acid. This kills fish, even if they appear to swim away unscathed.

➢ Handle the fish carefully. Use a wide-mouthed net to minimise handling or release the fish without lifting it out of the water. Some landing nets now have a scale built into the handle to minimise the handling of fish being weighed. Wet your hands well first, avoid touching the gill area, do not squeeze the stomach and take care not to rub off scales. A nylon stocking used as a glove can provide an excellent grip on the fish. Turning the fish upside down will often stop it struggling.

➢ Use artery forceps or slim-jawed pliers to remove hooks.

➢ Use barbless hooks. Ordinary hooks can be adapted by carefully crimping down the barb with slim-jawed pliers.

➢ Release the fish as quickly as possible. Some photographers keep fish out of the water far too long, considerably reducing their chance of recovery.

Anglers can assist fish and game councils and the Department of Conservation (DoC) by weighing and measuring all trout caught and supplying details from their diaries at the end of the season. This is especially important for fish that have been marked or tagged. Return tags to DoC along with the measurements. Metal or plastic tags are generally attached to, or near, the dorsal fin, and fish may also be marked by fin clipping or fin removal. Measure the fish's length from the fork of the tail to the tip of the snout. Record the species, weight, length and time and location of capture. Angler cooperation is vital in managing a fishery.

Regulations

Fishing regulations as stated in each section are current at time of print. Please note: to protect and enhance fisheries, the Fish and Game Council may modify the season and restriction on various waters.

Etiquette

This boils down to common courtesy towards landowners and other anglers.

Farmers will generally grant access to fishing water if you ask first; but they may get angry if they find people on their land who have not bothered to ask for permission.

Leave gates as you found them, whether closed or open. Avoid climbing over gates but, if you must, do so close to the hinges – climbing over the swinging end puts extra pressure on the hinges and damages them. Preferably climb through fences, not over them, as standing on the wires can damage them. If you decide to keep a fish for eating, clean it away from the water and bury the guts well.

Fires, firearms, dogs and rubbish are all absolute no-nos. Avoid disturbing stock and, if possible, call in to say thanks on the way out.

Failure to follow these simple rules will spoil it for others – and, in the long run, for everyone.

Angling etiquette varies depending on where you are fishing and the method used. For example, fishing the Tongariro River for run fish is entirely different from sight fishing a South Island spring creek. Disturbing trout intent on spawning can sometimes be beneficial from an angling viewpoint – although not all anglers will agree. Not so on a spring creek, where disturbed fish may sulk for 24 hours or more before resuming feeding.

On the Tongariro, first determine whether anglers are fishing upstream or downstream. If in doubt, ask those already fishing where you can join in. Never start fishing a pool upstream when anglers are fishing downstream, or vice versa. Do not remain stationary in the hot spot – keep moving through the pool to give others a chance. When an angler hooks a fish, reel in and leave plenty of room. After landing the fish, the angler should be allowed to rejoin the line at the spot he or she left it.

The same courtesy applies when fishing a stream mouth. Always join the end of the line unless there is an obvious gap, and even then, ask the other anglers whether it is permissible to fish in that spot. Do not disturb other anglers' water by excessive wading or walking out in front of where they are fishing. Do not impede other anglers' backcasts by walking too close behind.

When walking up a river and fishing for sighted fish, give other anglers who are already there at least 3–4 km of river to fish. Many overseas anglers do not realise that the fish population per kilometre of river can be very low in New Zealand. It is a good day's fishing if an angler spots 20 fish in a high-country stream. Do not duck into the bush and suddenly reappear to fish a few hundred metres upstream. If you have travelled a long way to fish this river, approach the other angler with a view to sharing the water or even fishing together. Often it is best simply to find another river.

An angler's unethical behaviour can sometimes be due to ignorance so it pays to check first before venting your wrath. There is nothing more certain to ruin your day's fishing than a confrontation on the river.

Useful information

☐ REGIONAL FISH & GAME COUNCILS

North Island

Eastern: Private Bag 3010, Rotorua, ph (07) 357 5501

Wellington (Wairarapa): Box 1325, Palmerston North, ph (06) 359-0409

Tongariro/Taupo Conservancy: Private Bag, Turangi, ph (07) 386-8607

South Island

Nelson/Marlborough: Box 2173, Stoke, ph (03) 544-6382
West Coast: Box 179, Hokitika, ph (03) 755-8546
Central South Island: Box 150, Temuka, ph (03) 615-8400
Otago: Box 76, Dunedin, ph (03) 477-9076
Southland: Box 159, Invercargill, ph (03) 215-9177

☐ **WEATHER FORECAST** (99 cents per minute)

Met Phone 0900 999 + area code:

- 09 Auckland
- 07 Bay of Plenty
- 04 Wellington
- 03 South Island

☐ **THE INTERISLANDER** (Cook Strait ferry)

Toll free 0800 802 802

☐ **METRIC TO US EQUIVALENTS**

1 kilometre (km) = 0.62 miles (km x 0.62 = miles)
1 litre (l) = 0.26 US gallon

☐ **WEIGHTS & MEASURES**

Metric measures and equivalents

- 1 centimetre (cm) = 0.39 in
- 1 kilogram (kg) = 2.2 lb

US measures and equivalents

- 1 inch (in) = 2.54 cm
- 1 pound (lb) = 0.4536 kg

☐ **TEMPERATURES**

Celsius to Fahrenheit: multiply by 1.8 then add 32
Fahrenheit to Celsius: subtract 32 then multiply by .55

°C	°F	°C	°F
0	32	40	104
5	41	45	113
10	50	50	122
15	59	60	140
20	68	80	176
25	77	100	212
30	86	120	248
35	95		

☐ VISITOR INFORMATION NETWORK

Visitor information centres provide comprehensive local information, including:

- accommodation listings and bookings
- transport information and booking
- itinerary planning and advice
- information on sightseeing and local attractions
- guide to restaurants
- gifts and souvenirs
- stamps and phonecards

North Island

AUCKLAND: Visitor Information Centre, 287 Queen St, PO Box 7048, ph (09) 979-2333, www.aucklandnz.com
There are also visitor centres at both the domestic and international terminals at Auckland Airport.

ROTORUA: Tourism Rotorua, 1167 Fenton St, PO Box 3007, ph (07) 348-5179, info@tourism.rdc.govt.nz

TAUPO: Visitor Centre, 30 Tongariro St, PO Box 865, ph (07) 376-0027, taupovc@lake tauponz.com

WAIRARAPA: Tourism Wairarapa, PO Box 814, Masterton, ph (06) 378-7373, tourwai@xtra.co.nz

WELLINGTON: Information Centre, 101 Wakefield St, PO Box 11007, ph (04) 802-4860

South Island

NELSON: Visitor Information Centre, PO Box 194, Nelson, ph (03) 548-2304, vin@latitudenelson.co.nz

BLENHEIM: Information Centre, PO Box 880, Blenheim, ph (03) 578-9904, blm-info@clear.net.nz

CHRISTCHURCH: Visitor Centre, Cathedral Square, PO Box 2600, ph (03) 379-9629.
There is also an information centre in the domestic terminal at Christchurch International Airport.

DUNEDIN: Visitor Centre, 48 The Octagon, PO Box 5457, ph (03) 474-3300

GORE: Information Centre, PO Box 1, Hokonui Heritage Village, Norfolk St, Gore, ph (03) 208-9908, goreinfo@esi.co.nz

GREYMOUTH: Information Centre, PO Box 95, ph (03) 768-5101

WANAKA: Visitor Information Centre, PO Box 147, Wanaka, ph (03) 443-1233, info@lakewanaka.co.nz

QUEENSTOWN: Visitor Information Centre, PO Box 353, Queenstown, ph (03) 442-4100, qvc@xtra.co.nz

Other local information centres are listed under each district.

☐ NEW ZEALAND PROFESSIONAL FISHING GUIDES ASSOCIATION INC. MEMBERS

The NZPFGA is New Zealand's national fishing guiding organisation. It represents the interests of guided anglers and the guiding industry as a whole. Membership criteria are set at a high level. Members must adhere to the highest ideals, and demonstrate this by financial contribution and by being actively involved, through advocacy, in furthering angling ethics, standards and sustainable management of New Zealand's fisheries.

For a full list of members of the NZPFGA, see the Appendix.

Fly fishing equipment

☐ LICENCE

To fish all waters in New Zealand except in the Taupo region, anglers must have a New Zealand licence. To fish in the Taupo region, a Taupo fishing licence is required (this does not apply to other regions).

At time of print, a licence costs around NZ$80.

☐ TACKLE

The brown and rainbow trout in New Zealand are large by world standards. As the climate is unpredictable and the days often windy, equipment will need to be tailored to meet these demands. Long casting is rarely required but an accurate first cast into a head wind is often essential.

☐ BASIC EQUIPMENT

Clippers	Forceps
Fly floatant	Landing net
Indicator material	Scales
Fishing vest	Hat
Polarised sunglasses	Rain jacket

Wading boots and gaiters	Camera and film
Woollen socks	Water bottle
Neoprene socks (optional)	Thermos
Day pack	Insect repellent
Sunscreen and lip balm	

☐ SMALL AND MEDIUM-SIZED RIVERS

Fly rod: 5–7 weight
Reel plus extra spools
Lines: floating line (preferably weight forward and dark in colour), sink-tip line
Leaders: 2.5–4.5 m (9–14 ft), tapered
Tippet nylon: 1.5–3 kg (3–6 lb)

Flies

Aquatic insects such as caddis, mayfly and stonefly larvae are the main trout food. During the summer months terrestrials such as the brown and green manuka beetles, cicadas and hoppers play a major role in the food chain.

We suggest the following assortment of flies but understand there will be personal preferences. It is also wise to visit local fly shops or sports stores to obtain up-to-date local information.

NYMPHS

Sizes 8–16

- Bead heads with some tungsten heads (a wide selection)
- Pheasant Tail
- Hare & Copper
- Hare's Ear
- Stonefly (green, black and brown)

DRY FLIES

Sizes 10–16

Adams (parachute favoured)	Humpy
Royal Wulff	Hoppers
Stimulators	Irresistible
Twilight Beauty	Dad's Favourite
Elk Hair Caddis	Coch-y-bondhu
Green Beetle	Black Gnat

A small selection of emerger patterns, soft-hackle wets, and well weighted Woolly Buggers would also be advisable.

☐ **LARGE RIVERS (TONGARIRO), LAKES AND STREAM MOUTHS**

Fly rod: 7–9 weight
Reel plus extra spools
Lines: weight forward floating, medium sink and shooting heads or Teeny 200
Leaders: 2.5–4.5 m (9–14 ft), tapered
Tippets: 2–4.5 kg (5–10 lb)
Waders: neoprene

LURES FOR STREAM-MOUTH AND LAKE FISHING

Rabbit flies (yellow and orange)
Smelt patterns: Grey Ghost, Parson's Glory, Doll Fly

LURES (WET FLIES) FOR RUN FISH (April–September)

Orange Rabbit
Red Setter

LURES FOR NIGHT FISHING AT STREAM MOUTHS

Hairy Dog
Fuzzy Wuzzy
Craig's Night-time
Black Marabou (with or without Aurora skirt)

NYMPHS FOR FISHING TO RUN FISH IN RIVERS

Hare & Copper (well weighted)
Flashback
Glow Bug (weighted and unweighted)
Muppet
Bug Eye (heavily weighted)

Note that in the Taupo and Rotorua districts, no lead may be incorporated in the body of any fly larger than size 10. Split shot, cork or polystyrene indicators are illegal: only synthetic or natural yarn may be used.

Suggested itineraries

Planning an itinerary is challenging as the options are almost limitless. Generally, the South Island offers better summer dry-fly and nymph fishing to sighted fish in clear rivers, whereas the North Island has better lake, lure (wet fly), night and winter fishing. However, by following this guide an angler could happily spend three or four weeks in summer in the North Island fishing some excellent water with dry fly, nymph and lure.

Anglers wishing to combine a winter fishing and skiing holiday in New Zealand could spend most of their time fishing in the North Island but ski in the South Island. However, there is also good skiing at Mt Ruapehu.

In summer, the South Island has so much water to fish that an angler could spend three weeks in one location and still not cover all the water available; to fish the South Island you should plan to be there between the beginning of November and the end of March. Good fishing is possible in the North Island throughout most of the year.

Lakes Aniwhenua, Rotoiti, Tarawera, Otamangakau and Okataina and the Rangitikei River (all in the North Island) are likely venues for catching trophy rainbow trout. For trophy brown trout, the more remote South Island back country is the preferred location.

Note that our suggested itineraries are only a guide. Weather and other circumstances may well necessitate a change of plan.

☐ NORTH ISLAND

TWO OR THREE WEEKS IN WINTER (APRIL–JULY)

- Arrive Auckland and travel to Rotorua for the first week.
- Arrange a professional guide and fish lakes Rotorua, Rotoiti, Tarawera, Okataina and Aniwhenua; also the Rangitaiki and Horomanga rivers, and Wheao Canal.
- For the second week, travel to Taupo and Turangi and seek the assistance of a professional guide. Fish the Tongariro and Tauranga–Taupo rivers during the day with nymph or lure. Visit Lake Otamangakau (especially in April) and fish some Taupo stream mouths at night. Note: neoprene waders and warm gear required.

TWO OR THREE WEEKS IN SUMMER (NOVEMBER–MARCH)

- Arrive Auckland and travel to Rotorua. Suggest fishing the Rangitaiki and Ruakituri rivers and Lake Rotorua stream mouths (three or four days).
- Travel to Taupo. Try lakeshore smelt fishing to cruising rainbows, and stream-mouth lure fishing both day and night.
- Consider visiting the Rangitikei, Ngaruroro or Mohaka rivers by fixed-wing aircraft or helicopter for sighted dry-fly and

nymph fishing. Lake Otamangakau is worth visiting for trophy fish; a float-tube or boat is an advantage on this lake.

➢ Travel to the Wairarapa and fish dry-fly and nymph in the Upper Manawatu, Makuri and Mangatainoka rivers (four or five days).

□ SOUTH ISLAND

TWO OR THREE WEEKS IN SUMMER (NOVEMBER–MARCH)

➢ Arrive Christchurch and hire a car or campervan.

➢ Travel to Omarama, hire a professional guide and fish the rivers in this area dry-fly and nymph, according to weather conditions. This should include the Ahuriri, Hakataramea, Twizel and Tekapo rivers and Lake Benmore. One could spend weeks in this area but we suggest five days.

➢ Travel to Wanaka and fish lakes Wanaka and Hawea for cruising fish, and the Hunter River. At night in high summer, try the Clutha River with a sedge (five days).

➢ Travel to Te Anau and hire a professional guide. Depending on weather, fish the Mararoa, Upukerora, Oreti, Eglinton, Worsley and Clinton rivers. Ten days could be easily spent in this area. A trip to Milford Sound is highly recommended.

➢ As an alternative, we suggest flying into Nelson, booking a professional guide and fishing the Nelson, Murchison and Lake Brunner districts. Three weeks would pass very quickly in these areas.

For itineraries four weeks or longer both South Island suggestions could be combined with Gore and Queenstown also included.

To fish both North and South Islands a four-week visit would be a minimum in our opinion.

ROTORUA district

More information can be obtained from Tourism Rotorua

Mail: Private Bag 3007, 1167 Fenton St, Rotorua

Freephone: 0800 ROTORUA (0800 768678) or (07) 348-5179

Fax: (07) 348-6004

Email: info@tourism.rdc.govt.nz

Rotorua city, with a population of 65,000, lies in the Bay of Plenty in the northeastern part of the North Island and is a three-hour drive from Auckland. Rotorua is a tourist mecca and is world famous for its geothermal activity and Maori culture. The New Zealand Maori Arts and Crafts Institute is located here. It is only an hour's drive to Tauranga with its orchards and beaches, to Whakatane with its big-game fishing, and to Taupo.

In the Rotorua district there are many lakes, exotic and native forests, rivers and farms. The tourist attractions and cultural activities are diverse and include mudpools, erupting geysers, steam vents, farm shows, Maori crafts and cultural performances, bush walks and hot spas. Rotorua also has two excellent golf courses.

As overseas tourists flock to this region, accommodation is plentiful – including holiday parks, hotels, motels, backpackers, bed and breakfasts, homestays and farmstays – but bookings should be made well in advance. At Lake Aniwhenua basic lodging is also available, and along the Ruakituri Valley road some farmers rent out shearers' quarters to anglers.

On non-fishing days we recommend touring the New Zealand Maori Arts and Crafts Institute, attending a hangi (feast cooked in an earth oven) and concert, viewing the Waimangu Volcanic Valley, Rainbow Springs Wildlife Sanctuary, Te Whakarewarewa Thermal Reserve, and

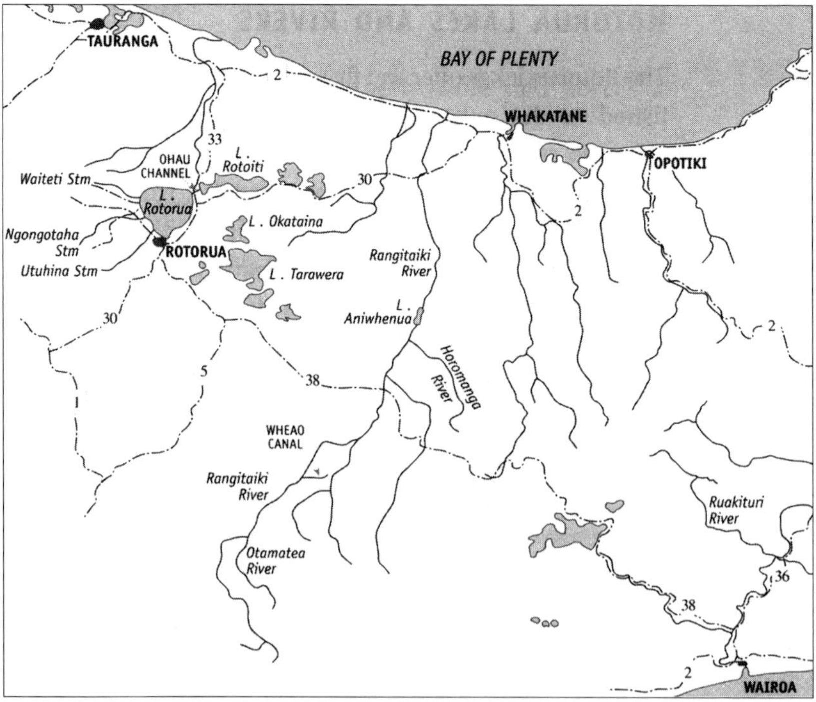

Rotorua district

the Buried Village, relaxing with a hot soak in the Polynesian Spa, and visiting the Waiotapu Thermal Wonderland and the Agrodome.

For the hiker, a walk around Lake Tikitapu (Blue Lake) or a stroll in the redwoods of the Whakarewarewa Forest can be most worthwhile. This area also offers a wide selection of attractive gardens and nurseries as the soil and climate produce magnificent rhododendrons, camellias and magnolias.

Rotorua's newly redeveloped city centre offers excellent shopping with easy parking and quality restaurants.

There are well stocked tackle shops in Rotorua and a number of professional trout fishing guides are available for hire.

R O T O R U A

Lakes and rivers

The Rotorua lakes offer wet fly (lure) and night fishing and are best fished in the autumn (fall), winter and spring months although stream-mouth fishing in summer when the lakes are warm can also be rewarding. Likewise, trolling, harling (trolling with a fly rod) and jigging are productive methods of catching good-sized trout. Lakes Rotoiti, Okataina, Tarawera and Aniwhenua offer every chance of landing a trophy trout.

The only river in this district within easy driving distance we would recommend is the Rangitaiki River. However, if helifishing is on the agenda, the Ruakituri River near Gisborne is well worth a visit.

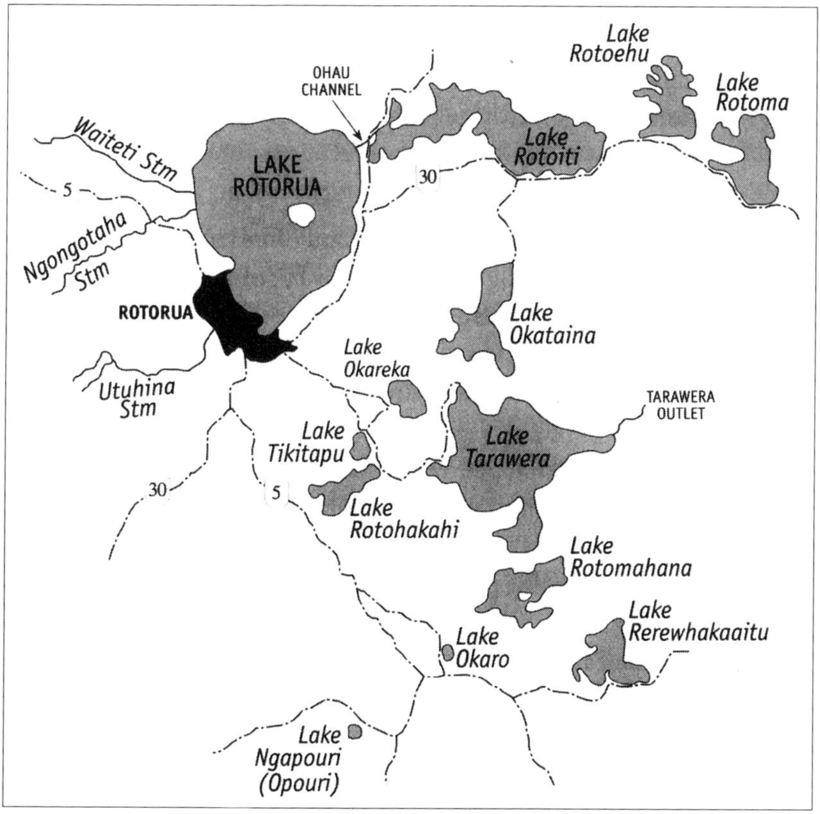

Rotorua lakes

TROUT FISHING REGULATIONS

- Fishing is prohibited between midnight and 5 am.
- Fly fishing only is permitted within 200 m of any stream mouth or outlet.
- Lake Rotokakahi (Green Lake) is privately owned and closed to fishing.
- Lead or wire lines may be used for trolling on all the Rotorua lakes excluding 'fly fishing only' areas. Downriggers with less than 40m of suspension cable are legal except on lakes Waikaremoana and Waikareiti.
- The daily bag limit in the Rotorua lakes is eight trout. Elsewhere, the limit is two trout.
- The daily limit for brown trout on lakes Waikaremoana, Rotorua, Tuai and Kaitawa is two trout.

LAKE ROTORUA

☐ Location and access

Rotorua city lies on the southern shore and access to the lake is generally freely available all around the lake.

☐ Season and restrictions

Except for the waters leading into the Ohau Channel, the lake is open for fishing all year. For streams flowing into the lake, 1 December–30 June.

☐ Boat ramps

These are numerous; the best all-weather ramp is at Sulphur Point through the Government Gardens. There are two at Hamurana, two at Ngongotaha, two in Rotorua and one at Hannahs Bay.

Lake Rotorua covers 7878 ha and is the largest lake in the district. However, it is relatively shallow – only 25 m maximum. Apart from the built-up areas, the lake is surrounded by farmland. There have been pollution problems in the past and in summer when the lake warms, a bloom of blue-green algae can be troublesome. Weed growth can be prolific in the shallow bays, but now that efforts are being made to improve the water quality, these problems will hopefully diminish. The shoreline and stream mouths are safe to wade. Good stocks of rainbow averaging 1.5 kg are present in the lake and, to add more interest, trophy browns up to 4 kg are not uncommon.

Fly fishing from the shore

When the lake temperature rises in summer, trout congregate in large numbers in the cooler, oxygenated water of stream mouths. Fishing can be excellent, especially at night from late December through to March. By April, trout begin their spawning runs and, although they can be caught, they do not congregate for any length of time before running upstream. Stream mouths are all shallow, so trout remain wary during the day unless the lake is ruffled by a stiff breeze. Fishing is best when this blows offshore.

Use a floating, slow-sinking or sink-tip line and a lure to imitate a smelt or bully. Lures to use during the day include smelt patterns, Rabbit varieties, Dorothy, Parson's Glory, Kilwell No 1, Lord's Killer and Hamill's Killer. At night, try Craig's Night-time, Scotch Poacher, Fuzzy Wuzzy, Hairy Dog, Black Prince and Black Maribou. Some anglers use two flies: a conventional black lure behind a Luminous Doll Fly. Small nymphs will take fish, but these are more effective in the lower reaches of the streams entering the lake.

On bright sunny summer days try wading out into the lake and looking back to shore. Using polarised sunglasses, large cruising browns can be spotted and stalked with a small smelt pattern or nymph. A favourite spot for this type of fishing is between Hamurana and the Ohau Channel, as the cliff background eliminates glare on the water and improves visibility. Cast well ahead of cruising fish.

Spinning can be carried out from shore, provided you are 200 m from any stream mouth. Flycasting from an anchored boat is also permitted at stream mouths and can be most rewarding when the lake is warm, but be sure to give shoreline anglers plenty of room.

Stream mouths

UTUHINA: Access from Arataua Street. Sunken boulders and logs snag a few deeply sunk lures.

NGONGOTAHA: Access from the end of Beaumonts Road or Taui Street by walking along the beach. Best when the wind blows from the west.

WAITETI: Access from Arnold or Operiana streets. Wading is possible out to 200 m at this shallow mouth. There is also good fishing in the slow-flowing lower reaches either side of the footbridge. Use a slow-sinking line and a black lure after dark or a small well sunk nymph during the day.

AWAHOU: Access from Gloucester Street. Considered to be the most productive stream mouth and heavily fished in January and February. Best in west or northwest winds.

HAMURANA: The mouth of this cold, spring-fed creek offers good fishing when the lake is warm. Closed upstream of the road bridge.

Other small stream mouths include the Waiowhiro, Waikuta, Waiohewa and Waingaehe (Holdens Bay Stream). These will take only two or three rods and fish best with an offshore breeze, a floating line and false casting. Some require permission from landowners. These streams are closed upstream from the mouth.

Trolling, jigging and harling

Except in the hot summer months, when fish gather round the cooler stream mouths, trolling and harling are very productive. More than half the trout caught in Lake Rotorua are landed from boats. Fish can be caught anywhere in the lake, although round Mokoia Island is a favourite area. Other spots worth trying are Kawaha Point, Sulphur Point, Hinemoa Point, the Airport Straight, Whakatane turnoff and in the vicinity of the Ohau Channel outlet. Early morning and late afternoon are the best times. When harling a fly, use a high-density sinking fly line or a colour or two of lead line if extra depth is required. The same flies as are recommended for stream mouths can be used for trolling, with the addition of Ginger Mick and Green or Yellow Orbit.

When trolling a spinner try black or green Cobra, Billy Hill, Tasmanian Devil, Black Toby or Flatfish. Blue, green and black are favoured colours. In rough conditions the lake can be treacherous, so keep a weather eye open.

ROTORUA STREAMS

☐ **Season and restrictions**

The Ngongotaha, Waiteti, Hamurana and Awahou streams are open all year below the bridges where the Ngongotaha and Hamurana roads cross them. The Utuhina below Lake Road bridge is also open all year. Upstream from these road bridges, the season is 1 December–30 June.

The Utuhina above the Pukehangi Road bridge and the Hamurana and Awahou streams above the Hamurana Road bridge are closed to fishing.

Fly fishing only is permitted on these streams below these bridges, with spin fishing allowed on the Utuhina Stream below the Devon Street bridge. Fly fishing only is permitted on the Awahou and Hamurana streams.

UTUHINA STREAM: Crossed by SH 5 near Ohinemutu. There are a number of accessways available through Rotorua City Council reserves.

NGONGOTAHA STREAM: Access off Ngongotaha Valley Road through private property. There are signposted access points.

WAITETI STREAM: The lower reaches can be reached from a footbridge near the mouth. The river here is slow-flowing and fishes better at night with a slow-sinking line and black lure. Access to the upper reaches is through private farmland north of Ngongotaha.

All are spawning streams for Lake Rotorua and hold good stocks of trout either early or late in the season. They are small, clear streams and, apart from in their lower reaches, fish can be stalked and easily spooked. Although overgrown in parts, some sections offer good small-nymph fishing for run fish in May and June or for a few post-spawning fish early in December.

OHAU CHANNEL

☐ Location

Flows slowly and deeply between Lake Rotorua and Lake Rotoiti. Crossed by SH 30.

☐ Access

Much of the land bordering the channel is held by Maori, and permission should be sought. The Ohau Channel Camp proprietor will allow access to the camp area, except on opening day when only anglers staying at the camp have permission.

☐ Season and restrictions

1 October–30 June. Fly fishing only. Fishing is not permitted from an anchored boat within 200 m of the entrance or exit. Bag limit is eight trout.

Trout live, spawn and migrate through this channel at certain times of the year. Lake Rotoiti trout have very little natural spawning area so many pass through the channel on their way to spawn in the Rotorua streams. In spring and early summer schools of smelt also migrate through the channel and attract trout. Because the water is deep, a sinking line should be used, and cast well across and upstream to allow the lure to sink before commencing the retrieve. The most heavily fished section is near the weir at the Rotorua end. The best time is early and late in the season: October–November and May–June are prime months. Rainbow and brown trout averaging 2 kg can be expected, with a few trophy fish caught each season.

During the day try smelt patterns such as Grey Ghost, Ginger Mick, Hawk and Silver, Doll Fly, Dorothy, Yellow and Silver Rabbit and Jack Spratt. At night use the usual night patterns like Black Maribou, Black Prince, Craig's Night-time, Fuzzy Wuzzy, Scotch Poacher and luminous flies. Late in the season when fish spawn in the channel, some anglers have success with egg patterns.

OHAU DELTA

☐ **Location**

This is the exit or mouth of Ohau Channel into Lake Rotoiti.

☐ **Access**

From SH 33 at the rest area 1.5 km east of Mourea.

☐ **Season and restrictions**

1 October–30 June. Bag limit is eight trout.

Wading can be tricky as the bottom is uneven. The lip is deep and drops off suddenly. Stand back 10 m or so from the lip and cast over it with a sinking line. Wait until your lure sinks, then quietly retrieve. April, May and June are the best months. Few anglers fish here at night, although there is no apparent reason for this except perhaps the difficulties in wading. It would pay to be in position before dark. Use similar flies as for the Ohau Channel with the addition of Hamill's Killer, Kilwell No 1 and Mrs Simpson.

LAKE ROTOITI

☐ **Location**

Lies northeast of Lake Rotorua. Rotoiti is the third largest lake in the Rotorua area and covers 3340 ha. The northern shore is bushclad.

☐ **Access**

SH 30 follows the southern shore and SH 33 the western shore. Large areas of this lake can be reached only by boat.

☐ **Season and restrictions**

From 1 October to 30 June. There is an open season for shoreline anglers between landmarks situated at Ruato and Hinehopu and extending 200 m offshore. Trolling is not permitted within this area. Bag limit is eight trout.

☐ **Boat launching**

There are boat ramps at Otaramarae, Waipuna Bay, Gisborne Point and Hinehopu. Otaramarae is the deepest.

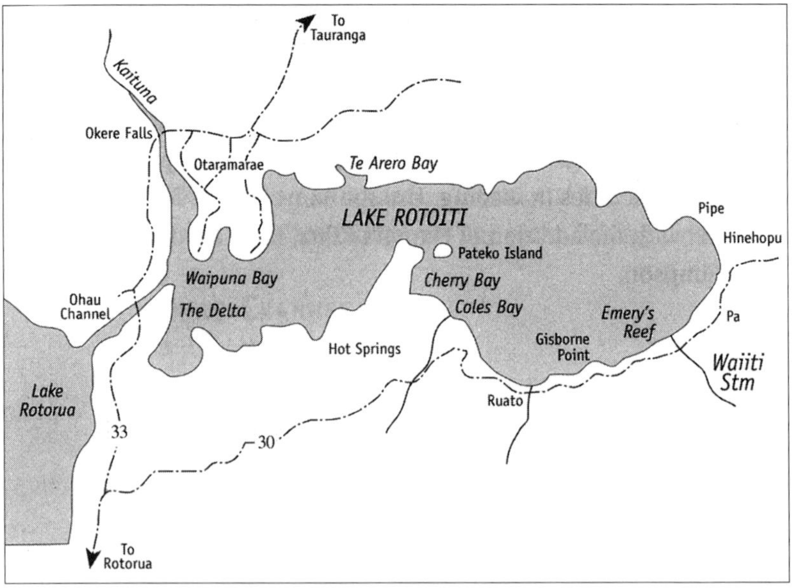

Lake Rotoiti

Fly fishing

Regular releases of Ngongotaha Hatchery 'R' type rainbow fry are made along the shore between Ruato Bay and Hinehopu. These fish have been selectively bred for rapid growth and large potential size. When mature, they return to their release site to spawn along the shallow, sandy beaches, and provide good shoreline fly fishing, especially at night from April to the end of October. Fish weighing over 4.5 kg are not uncommon.

Fishing pressure can be intense at times, with some anglers securing their spot well before dark. The same shoreline can be fished during the day but trout are shy and much more difficult to catch. Most fish are caught in shallow water close to shore, so quiet wading, false casting and a slow retrieve are required. Use a floating sink-tip or slow-sinking line and during the day try Red Setter, Kilwell No 1, Hamill's Killer, Mrs Simpson, Parson's Glory, Jack Spratt and egg patterns. At night try Scotch Poacher, Black Phantom, Hairy Dog, Black Marabou and Luminous Doll Fly. Many anglers use two flies at night, one with a luminous body.

When fishing Rotoiti it is wise to have 100 m of backing on your reel as, although some fish are disappointing fighters, others hardly ever stop.

The following shoreline spots are recommended.

HAUPARU BAY: This is the first bay reached from Rotorua on SH 30. Access is down a driveway opposite the bus stop. A small stream mouth is 30 m down the beach to your right. Note that this bay closes on 30 June as wild fish spawn in the stream.

RUATO (TWIN STREAM) BAY: SH 30 runs the length of this popular bay and the odd logging truck has been caught on the backcast. Two streams enter the lake, one at each end of the sandy beach; the larger stream, at the east end, provides the better fishing. An offshore wind is desirable and wading is often unnecessary, especially late at night. Fish are taken close in on floating lines. If the fishing is still slow by 9.30 pm it is probably not worth persisting.

EMERY'S REEF: This spot is opposite Emery's Store. Enter the lake on the right-hand side of the jetty and wade quietly along the shore for 80 m to a large karaka tree on the bank above. There is an old engine block to stand on, if you can find it. The reef can be covered by casting out slightly to your left. A cold spring near the reef attracts fish.

GISBORNE POINT: Wade still further along the shore from Emery's Reef to the point. There is another cold spring, close to the shore.

WAIITI STREAM: SH 30 crosses this stream. Access to the mouth is from the eastern side of the bridge. It fishes best in windy conditions, especially a northerly, with room for four or five rods.

QUARRY (DUMP): The quarry and rubbish collection area can be seen from SH 30 and access is easy from the road to the lake. The lake fishes well in a westerly all along this shoreline, from the quarry past 'The Transformer' and 'The Pipe' to the bluff at Hinehopu. There is good safe wading.

THE PIPE: Lies at the far end of the beach past the baches at Hinehopu. Fishes best after rain, when water flows through the pipe from the swamp behind. Wading should be avoided and a slow or medium-sinking line used. Cast over the drop-off and wait a while before slowly retrieving. There is also good fishing beyond the pipe towards the bush-covered bluff, but wading is necessary to avoid snagging the bush on the backcast. Watch for slippery sunken logs along the sandy beach.

Trolling and harling

A lot of fish are caught trolling a spinner or harling a fly from a boat. Popular areas include the northern bushclad shore, Sulphur Bay, Pateko Island, Cherry Bay, Coles Bay and Te Arero Bay. Harling a fly over weed beds on a high-density fly line is often more effective than trolling 'hardware'. The cooler months of the year and early morning and late evening are the best times. Try Parson's Glory, Orange and Green Rabbit, Red Setter and Green Orbit lures and Tasmanian Devil, Cobra, Billy Hill, Pearl or Toby spinners. Black and red are popular colours.

Jigging and ledgering are popular along the northern shore. Tie your boat up to an overhanging branch.

In winter, try the Rotoiti hot pools on the edge of the lake and don't forget to jump off the jetty to cool down!

LAKE TARAWERA

☐ Location and access

Lies southeast of Rotorua city. Turn right off SH 30 at Ngapuna and drive 15 km, past the Blue Lake and Buried Village, to the lake. The outlet can be reached through the Tasman forest from Kawerau (a permit is required from the forestry manager).

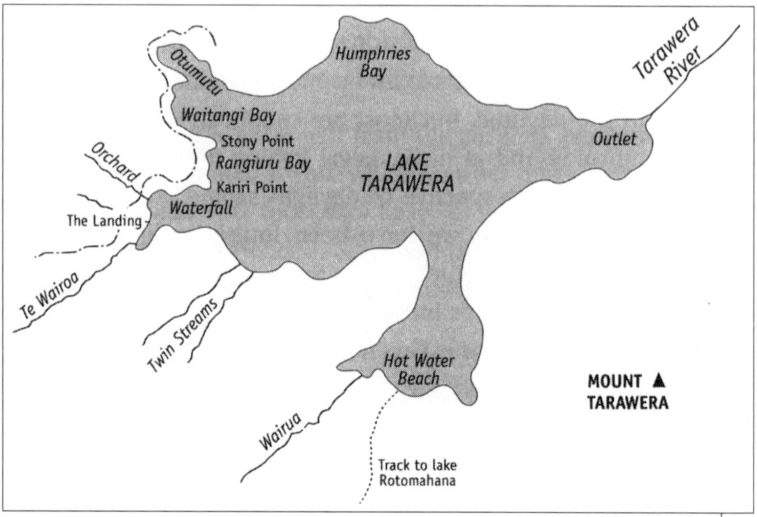

Lake Tarawera

☐ Season and restrictions

Open for fly fishing all year between the landmark at the southern end of the Te Wairoa Landing (excluding the Te Wairoa Stream mouth) and the landmark on the northern side of the Otumutu Lagoon and extending 200 m offshore, and between the Tarawera outlet and the landmark at the southern end of Te Tapahoro Bay. Elsewhere, 1 October–30 June. Lake Tarawera outlet is closed to fishing for 150 m downstream. Below this spawning sanctuary, fly fishing only is permitted.

Fly fishing only is permitted within 200 m of all stream mouths and at The Landing.

Catch and release for all wild rainbow trout measuring over 65 cm in length and all male fish caught within 200 m of the Te Wairoa Stream mouth. Bag limit is eight trout.

☐ Boat launching

Ramps are located at Te Wairoa Landing, Stony Point Reserve, Kariri Point boatsheds, Rangiuru Bay, Otumutu and Te Tapahoro.

Lake Tarawera has always seemed a dark, forbidding lake. It is very deep and dominated by the now dormant volcanic Mt Tarawera. Bushclad hills surround most of the shoreline and in winter Tarawera can be very cold and inhospitable. The lake can cut up rough during a strong southerly or even an easterly, so boat owners be warned.

In the past, the lake has been renowned for its trophy rainbow but now it is unusual to land a fish weighing over 4.5 kg. However, the measures taken by the Eastern Fish and Game Council, as outlined in the restrictions, will hopefully restore this fishery to its former glory.

Shoreline fly fishing

Stream mouths are favoured spots during April, May and June, but angling pressure can be intense. Some fish can be taken during the day but most are caught at change of light or at night. Favoured lures for daytime fishing include Kilwell No 1, Red Setter, Hamill's Killer, Leslie's Lure, Green Smelt and Parson's Glory, in sizes 6–8. At night try Scotch Poacher, Black Marabou, Fuzzy Wuzzy, Black Prince and Luminous Doll Fly.

The following are favoured spots.

TE WAIROA STREAM MOUTH: Follow the track to the right from the Te Wairoa Landing for 150 m. The stream mouth holds five or six rods, but care is needed when wading as the drop-off is very deep. Stand back and fish quietly over the lip. At night, use a medium-sinking line but during the day a fast sinker or even a shooting head is best. There is a weed bank to the right and at night or early in the morning fish can be taken on a floating line over this bank. Fishes best in a westerly or southwesterly. Remember that jack fish must be released; this can be a problem for anglers fishing the 'heave and leave' method as trout swallow the egg pattern well down the gullet and are often left bleeding after the hook is removed.

MAIN BEACH OR LANDING: Turn off the Tarawera Road onto Spencer Road. During an easterly, and especially late in the season, anglers crowd this beach shoulder to shoulder as schools of fish move close into the stirred-up waves. Many of the fish caught will be foul-hooked and must be released. Use a slow-sinking line and a Red Setter or killer pattern during the day and one of the usual night lures at night.

THE JETTIES: Use a medium to fast-sinking line off the jetties but a floater if fishing the tiny stream mouth to the left of the jetty. Best at night and in westerly conditions.

THE ORCHARD: Walk to the left from the carpark beneath the rocky bluff to a small stream that empties into shallow water. Holds only two rods, and false casting with a floating line is required so as not to frighten fish. Start well back as fish move close in during early morning and at dusk. Best in a westerly.

RANGIURU BAY: Drive past Spencer Road to Rangiuru Road. This leads to a picnic area and boat ramp by the willows. Wading is necessary; the most popular spot is in the southwest corner. There is a broad sandy shelf out in front of a bush-covered promontory with acacia trees on the skyline. Wade out 40 m and fish over the lip with a medium-sinking line. Fish can be taken during the day, but night fishing provides the best sport. Use the usual black night flies dressed with or without Aurora skirt, and a Luminous Doll Fly. It pays to carry a landing net as it is a long walk back to shore. Fishes best in a westerly or southwesterly.

WAITANGI BAY: Access to this spot is from the end of Waitangi

Road. Follow a path to the foreshore reserve and round into the bay. As conditions are similar to the Orchard, use a floating line with false casting.

THE WATERFALL: Enters Te Wairoa Bay beyond the Orchard and can only be fished by casting from an anchored boat.

TWIN STREAMS: Access by boat between Te Wairoa Bay and the Wairua Arm. Cast from an anchored boat or wade the shelf and fish over the lip.

WAIRUA STREAM MOUTH: Access is by boat to the head of Wairua Arm. Can offer great fishing at times from April to June but is heavily fished. Best at night and comfortably holds three rods, but this is a rare event these days. Fish school off the mouth before running up the stream to spawn. Cast over the lip where the stream melts into the lake, using a medium-sinking line. During the day try Orange Rabbit, Kilwell No 1, Red Setter or a small smelt pattern. At night use Black Maribou, Scotch Poacher, Black Prince, Hairy Dog, Fuzzy Wuzzy or Red Setter. A Luminous Doll Fly sometimes works well.

Trolling and harling

Harling a Yellow Rabbit or Parson's Glory along the lip or over shelves can be exciting early in the season, but when the weather warms trolling with a wire or lead line is necessary. Fish can be caught anywhere, although Humphries Bay is popular. Early morning and late evening are the best times. It is a matter of finding the fish and fishing at the right depth. Favoured spinners include Flatfish, Tasmanian Devil, Toby, Cobra and Zed.

LAKE OKATAINA

☐ Location and access

Turn right off SH 30 at Ruato and travel 6 km along a scenic bush-lined road to the lake.

☐ Season and restrictions

There is an open season for shoreline fishing from landmarks situated at Te Koutu Point and west of Okataina Lodge. Elsewhere, 1 October–30 June.

Fly fishing only within 200 m of any stream mouth. Bag limit is eight trout.

☐ **Boat ramp**
At Home (Tauranganui) Bay.

This beautiful, deep, unspoiled lake is surrounded by native bush. Since the introduction of 'R' type rainbows, this lake and Lake Rotoiti have become the trophy lakes of the Rotorua district. Fish weighing over 6 kg have been caught by flycasting from the shore and fishing from a boat. You will need 100 m of backing on your reel. As with Lake Rotoiti, there are few spawning streams entering the lake, so fish move into the shallows during the colder months in search of spawning beds.

When flycasting from the shore during the day, use a slow or medium-sinking line, but at night use a floater. Some wading is required and is safe. Fish can be taken anywhere along the shore, especially during April, May and June. The best times are early morning, dusk and at night. Prime spots are stream mouths, the Log Pool, Te Koutu (Maori) Point, Rocky Point, Parimata and Kaiakahi bays. As is usual in the Rotorua lakes, fish go deep during January, February and March and shoreline fishing becomes very difficult.

If fishing from an anchored boat, use a high-density or shooting-head line and fish deep over the weed beds. Popular lures include smelt and rabbit patterns, Green Hairy Dog, Parson's Glory and Red Setter. At night pukeko night flies (eg, Scotch Poacher, Craig's Night-time) are effective along with a Luminous Doll Fly. Some anglers have success ledgering a Muppet or Glow Bug.

When trolling or harling, the secret for success in this lake is to get down deep. Lead or wire lines are generally used, although early in the morning or at dusk fish can be caught harling a fly on a high-density line over weed beds. Popular spinners are Toby, Flatfish, Cobra, Penny and Tasmanian Devil.

RANGITAIKI RIVER

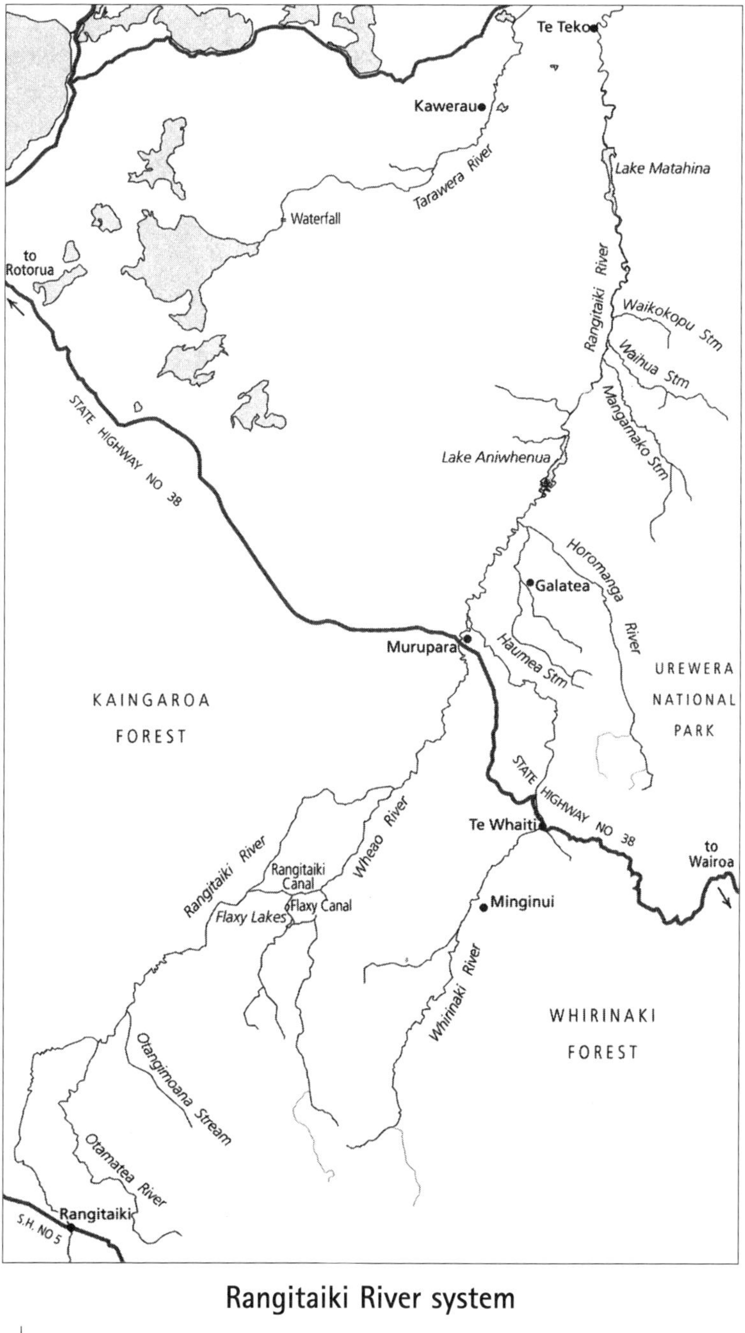

Rangitaiki River system

This large river rises on Lochinvar Station then flows north beneath SH 5 (the Napier–Taupo road) just east of Rangitaiki. From SH 5 the river meanders through the Kaingaroa exotic forest to Murupara, then across the Galatea Plains to the hydro Lake Aniwhenua.

Further north, the river enters and leaves another hydro Lake Matahina. From the Matahina Dam, the river continues its northerly course across farmland to enter the sea near Thornton. The river has been modified by four hydroelectric powerstations. For convenience the river can be divided into three sections: upper, middle and lower, but the lower reaches are not worth exploring with a fly rod.

Upper reaches (Kaingaroa Forest)

☐ Location

From SH 5 (the Napier–Taupo road) bridge. There is a small section of river upstream from the bridge that can be fished with a spinner, but generally this section is overgrown with scrub.

☐ Access

Downstream access off SH 5 is via Low Level and River roads to the Otamatea confluence. Below this confluence, Eastern Boundary Road follows the river to the Te Awa Camping Ground.

From SH 38 (Rotorua–Murupara Road), take Wairapukao Road into Kaingaroa Forest, then Low Level Road and Wainuki Road to the Te Awa Camping Ground. Eastern Boundary Road follows upstream.

You will need a permit to access Kaingaroa Forest to fish the Rangitaiki River, the Rangitaiki (Wheao) Canal, Flaxy Lakes, Otamatea River, Otangimoana River and Wheao River. This permit can be obtained from the Fletcher Challenge Forests Visitor Centre, Long Mile Road, Rotorua, ph (07) 346-2082.

At times, in summer, the forest can be closed because of fire risk. We strongly suggest you get a map of the forest, as the forestry roads can be very confusing. Free basic camping is available at Te Awa at times when there is no fire risk.

From SH 38 just west of the Rangitaiki Bridge near Murupara, take Kiorenui Road to the Rangitaiki (Wheao) Canal. Bush Road leaves the southern side of the canal and gives access to the Flaxy lakes and Flaxy Canal. A branch road off Kiorenui Road, Ngahuinga Road leads to the Rangitaiki–Wheao river confluence.

☐ **Season and restrictions**

Above the Otamatea River confluence, 1 October–30 June. Below this confluence, the Rangitaiki River is open all year. Bag limit is two trout.

There is 25 km of highly regarded river to fish in the Kaingaroa Forest. The river is deep and slow-flowing in some stretches but there are a few riffles and runs. Although the brownish water is generally clear, trout are not easy to spot except from a high bank in bright light. With a pumice, shingle, rock and weed riverbed, wading is not too difficult and there are places where the river can be crossed. Some stretches are overgrown with scrub, tussock and toetoe (native grass) and difficult to fish. It can be tiresome retrieving flies from toetoe bushes more than 2 m high!

Fish rise readily to hatches, even during the day. Watch the rise form, as the insects may be emergers. The river holds a good stock of both brown and rainbow trout, with drift dives revealing 98 medium-sized rainbows per km of river and a smaller number of browns. There are a few fish of around 4 kg. November to March is the most popular time to visit this river although we had great sport one May when fish were frantically feeding on a mayfly hatch. Trout can be taken on dry flies, emergers, nymphs, soft-hackle wets and even lures fished deeply across and down.

Below the Wheao confluence there is good water all the way to SH 38, although much of the fishing is done with a spinning rod.

Middle reaches

☐ **Location and access**

Along the Murupara–Te Teko Road (Galatea), generally across private farmland.

☐ **Season and restrictions**

Open all year.

The river becomes very large, deep and slow-flowing here. Fishing can be difficult between the willows but there are some stretches that offer reasonable fly fishing and you are unlikely to encounter other anglers. There is a good rise on calm, warm summer evenings. Most of the fish are caught on spinning gear. Some anglers use a boat to access the river upstream from Lake Aniwhenua.

RANGITAIKI (WHEAO) CANAL

☐ **Location and access**

Kiorenui Road leaves SH 38 just west of the Rangitaiki Bridge near Murupara. Kiorenui Road crosses the canal, and roads run on both sides.

☐ **Season and restrictions**

Open all year. Bag limit is two trout.

This canal, which diverts Rangitaiki River water to the Wheao hydroelectric power scheme, is 20 m wide and 8 m deep in the middle. Fish get trapped in the canal by passing through the control gates and there is an abundance of insect life. Trout are hard to spot but there are good numbers of brown and rainbow up to 3 kg. There is a good evening rise in favourable conditions. Try mayfly and caddis imitations.

FLAXY LAKES

☐ **Location and access**

Bush Road off Kiorenui Road alongside the Rangitaiki-Wheao Canal leads to these two small lakes joined by a canal.

☐ **Season and restrictions**

Open all year. Bag limit is two trout.

These hydro lakes hold mainly rainbow trout, with some of trophy proportions. Best fished in the cooler months, especially near the creek mouth at the south end, where fish gather prior to spawning. Fishing can be slow in summer and patient anglers using small nymphs from a float-tube or small boat have the best opportunities. In summer, dry flies can be effective but in April, use a sinking line and a Woolly Bugger or Hamill's Killer.

Ngaruroro River.

Off you go!

Ruamahanga River.

Ruakituri River.

Makuri River.

Tauranga-Taupo River flood debris.

Waitahanui River.

Tongariro River lineup.

Silly Pool, Tongariro River.

Down and across on the Tongariro River.

Bright colourful rainbow.

Aqua stealth sole.

Boil the billy.

Cork handle acts as good insulator.

Captured brown beauty.

Can you spot the brownie?

LAKE ANIWHENUA

☐ Location

Lies on the Galatea Plains north of Murupara, Galatea and the confluence of the Horomanga and Rangitaiki rivers.

☐ Access

Southern end: From both sides of Rabbit Bridge.

Kopuriki Road: Access downstream from Rabbit Bridge on the eastern side.

Galatea Road: Access across private farmland.

Northern end: From Black Road to the free camping area and dam. A track follows the eastern shoreline south from the boat ramp.

☐ Season and restrictions

Open all year. Bag limit is two trout.

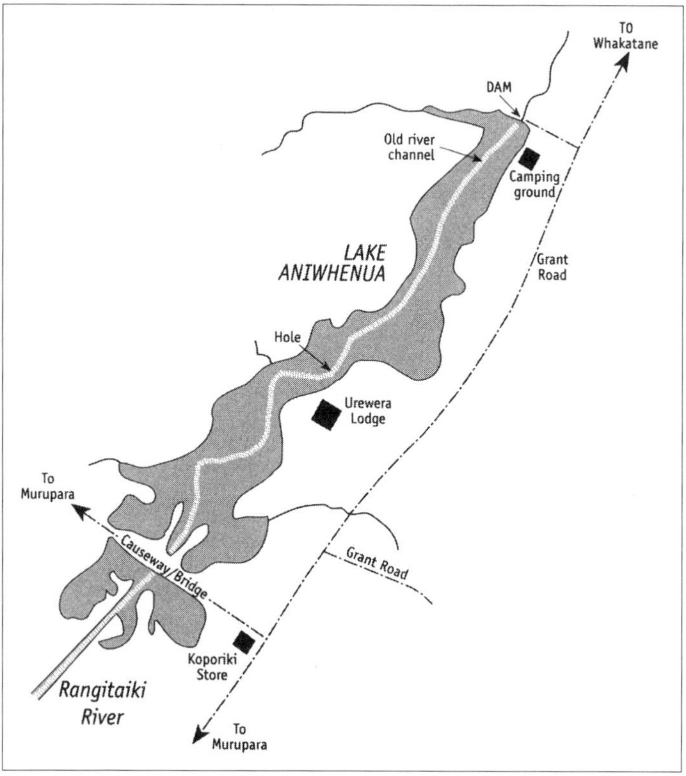

Lake Aniwhenua

☐ **Boat launching**

There are two ramps: at Rabbit Bridge and at the camping area off Black Road.

Formed in 1980, this hydro lake, covering 200 ha, averages only 2.5 m in depth, except for some deep holes along the old Rangitaiki riverbed. The eastern shoreline is farmland, while the western shore is scrub-covered and generally unfishable from the shore.

This is a lake for the trophy hunter, with large, wild rainbow and brown trout in good condition, up to 6 kg. Although it is easier to fish from a boat or float-tube, there is shoreline fishing at both ends of the lake and along the eastern shore. On a bright summer's day, browns especially can be spotted cruising the edges. By mid summer the lake has warmed and fish seek the colder, deeper waters of the old riverbed.

In the cooler months, the fishing tends to improve. Fish can be taken trolling, harling a fly, spinning, flycasting from the shore and night fishing using a large black lure. Flycasting from a drifting boat at night using a sinking line is the most productive method. The top spots are the old Rangitaiki riverbed holes. During the day, nymphs account for most fish caught.

Before 1996 net weed was a serious problem, especially for trollers, but in February 1996 it mysteriously disappeared. However, trout size diminished somewhat and it became apparent that net weed harboured thousands of worms, a high-protein diet for trout. It has been replaced by oxygen weed and red weed, and although trout feed on the snails living in these weeds, the worms were a better food source. The average weight of trout caught has dropped. Although oxygen weed regresses in winter there are still wild goldfish present and these are important trout food.

Flies to use on this productive lake include Hare and Copper and Dragonfly nymphs, Black and Peacock, olive-green and brown Woolly Bugger, Muddler Minnow and Hamill's Killer lures, and Cicada and Midge Pupa in summer. Dry flies are used but the main source of trout food is sub-surface. When all else fails, a San Juan Worm is worth trying. At night a Black Marabou, with or without Aurora skirt, is a good choice.

HOROMANGA RIVER

□ Location

Rises in the heavily bushclad hills of the Urewera National Park, flows in a northwesterly direction and joins the Rangitaiki River just above Lake Aniwhenua.

□ Access

Lower reaches are accessed where Galatea Road crosses the river, and middle reaches from the Troutbeck Road bridge. To access the upper reaches follow the gravel road running upstream on the true left bank from the south side of the Troutbeck Road bridge. A track continues upstream from the end of the gravel road. There are two DoC huts further upstream in the headwaters if you plan to stay overnight.

□ Season and restrictions

1 October–30 June. Fly fishing only is permitted on this river and its tributaries. The bag limit is two trout, but we recommend releasing all fish caught in the upper reaches.

This relatively small river holds a few good-sized resident fish in some deep pools in the upper reaches and headwaters. However, the main attraction is the spawning run of large fish. These enter from Lake Aniwhenua during April, May and June, but some late spawners are still present when the season opens on 1 October.

The lower reaches hold small resident rainbows and are shingly and relatively unstable. There are more stable, deeper pools in the middle and upper reaches, where trout can be spotted and stalked. A few patches of scrub along the banks make casting more difficult, but access to these stretches is generally good. The headwaters are bush-lined.

Most fish are caught on small weighted nymphs such as Hare and Copper, Hare's Ear, Pheasant Tail and Halfback. Some anglers use egg patterns like Glow Bug and Muppet. Although the bag limit is two fish, we believe all trout caught from this stream should be released so the gene pool for Lake Aniwhenua is maintained. Some large fish have been landed from this stream in seasons past.

RUAKITURI RIVER

☐ Location

It is a long and difficult drive from Rotorua to this river. However, if visiting Lake Waikaremoana it is worth the extra 90 minutes' drive to the Ruakituri Valley. This rather remote, highly recommended river drains the rugged, bushclad hills north of Lake Waikaremoana, flows southeast and joins the Hangaroa River at the spectacular Te Reinga Falls.

☐ Access

HEADWATERS: From Waimaha Station (obtain permission first), at the end of Taumata Road, west of Rere, via a farm track and a three-hour bush tramp on Rua's Track to the Anini Stream.

From Papuni Station: This lies at the end of Ruakituri Valley Road and Papuni Road. Ruakituri Valley Road leaves SH 36 at Te Reinga. After obtaining permission, take the farm track (paper road) to the road end at Lockwoods and the carpark. It is a two and a half to three-hour tramp to Waitangi Falls and the river above the falls.

To the Waipaoa tributary: Gained by fording the main river below Papuni Gorge and tramping upstream on the true right bank from Ruakituri Reserve. Papuni Station claims riparian rights, so the true left bank of the Ruakituri River is closed to fishing upstream from Makokomuka Ford as far as the Urewera National Park boundary at Flanagans Creek.

MIDDLE AND LOWER REACHES: Follow Ruakituri Valley Road upstream, at first on the true left and later on the true right bank, to Erepeti bridge. Papuni Road continues up on the true left to Papuni Station. There are numerous access points from this road, but ask permission to cross private farmland unless access is easy and obvious. There are a few campsites in the valley (with no facilities) and some local farmers rent out their shearers' quarters to anglers.

Do not attempt to fish through the Erepeti Gorge, immediately above the Erepeti Bridge, unless the river is low.

☐ Season and restrictions

1 October–30 June. Fly fishing only. The bag limit is two fish and,

above Waitangi Falls, only fish measuring less than 60 cm can be taken. There is no maximum length restriction below the falls. This relatively inaccessible, medium-sized river offers superb fly fishing for more than 30 km of main river. There is another 20 km of water in the headwaters and tributaries for anglers who are proficient in bushcraft and prepared to tramp.

Above Waitangi Falls, there are trophy rainbow up to 5 kg but you need to be fit, able to scramble round rocky bluffs and confident about fording rivers. Trout can be spotted but some of the pools are overgrown, deep and difficult to fish. Anglers intent on fishing above Waitangi Falls need to camp out in the bush in fine summer weather. If the Anini tributary is reached from Rua's Track, the best fishing lies downstream from where the track crosses the river.

The Waipaoa tributary upstream from Papuni Station is a delight to fish and again holds mainly rainbows, averaging 1.8 kg. This clear stream flows through partially cleared native bush and pastoral land, has well developed pools and extends 10 km upstream from its confluence with the Ruakituri. Again, you should consider tramping and camping to enjoy the best of this stream. Anglers prepared to tramp upriver beyond Lockwoods carpark and fish above where the Waitangi Falls track leaves the river will find excellent fishing in boisterous water for large fish.

The Papuni Gorge holds fish, as does the slow-flowing stretch of river above Papuni Station, but anglers must respect the riparian rights of the station.

For anglers keen on nymphing, the stretch of river between the Erepeti bridge and the Makokomuka Stream is hard to beat. Trout stocks are very high and fish average around 2 kg. Browns and rainbows are present in equal numbers but are not easy to spot unless the river is low or the fish are feeding on the edges of runs. The water often has a hint of colour and as this is rather unstable papa (mudstone) country, rain usually discolours the river and it may take three days to clear. The riverbed is papa, boulders, stones and silt, and wading anglers should be wary of the slippery rock and deep slots in it. There are well defined pools, but many fish hold behind rocks in the fast runs. Seldom are there any casting obstructions. The river can be crossed at the tail of most pools; a wading stick is helpful.

Below Erepeti bridge, there is excellent water all the way

downstream to below the Ruakituri School. The river is willow-lined in this section and trout are very difficult to spot. It is worth fishing all the likely-looking water with an attractor-pattern dry fly or well weighted nymph.

Most trout are caught in the Ruakituri on well weighted caddis and mayfly nymphs. The deeper runs should be fished with two nymphs and an indicator. On summer evenings there is often an active splashy caddis rise on some of the more quietly flowing pools. Try an Elk Hair or a Goddard Caddis in these conditions.

Trout fight hard in this river and rainbows will often test a 4 kg tippet. As the fish often have a muddy flavour, catch and release is recommended.

TONGARIRO–TAUPO conservancy

For more information contact:

TAUPO VISITOR CENTRE

Mail: PO Box 865, 30 Tongariro Street, Taupo

Phone: (07) 376-0027

Fax: (07) 378-9003

Email: taupovc@laketauponz.com

TURANGI VISITOR CENTRE

Mail: PO Box 34, Turangi

Phone: (07) 386-8999

Fax: (07) 386-0074

Email: turangi@laketauponz.com

Lake Taupo lies in the centre of the North Island and is a popular tourist destination. It is three and a half hours from Auckland and five hours from Wellington by car. There are scheduled daily bus services from many North Island cities and towns, and it is a one-hour flight from Auckland International Airport.

Taupo is a sophisticated tourist venue with modern accommodation, good restaurants and shopping facilities. There are two excellent golf courses, natural thermal spas and a host of other scenic attractions including two thermal areas close by, at Wairakei and Orakei Korako. In addition, Honey Hive New Zealand, the Huka Falls, and the world's only geothermally heated prawn farm are all within a 30-minute drive from the town centre. There are also scenic lake cruises, bush walks, and horse treks for non-fishing days.

Turangi, at the southern end of the lake, is a 40-minute drive from Taupo township and offers whitewater rafting, tramping and skiing in the Tongariro National Park, and a hot soak in the thermal spa at Tokaanu. The Tongariro National Trout Centre and hatchery, just south of Turangi, is worth a visit and can be combined with fishing the Birch pools on the Tongariro River nearby.

There are well stocked tackle shops in both Taupo and Turangi, and professional trout fishing guides are available for hire.

TAUPO DISTRICT TROUT

Ova from European brown trout (*Salmo trutta*) were brought to the South Island in 1867 from Tasmania (where they had earlier been acclimatised), and to Taupo in 1886. Rainbow trout (*Oncorhynchus mykiss*) ova from Sonoma Creek in California were obtained in 1883, hatched in a pond in the Auckland Domain and liberated in Lake Taupo in 1897. All the rainbow trout in New Zealand have originated from this one shipment.

Food in Lake Taupo was initially plentiful and included the banded kokupu and inanga (small native fishes which are the adult forms of whitebait), koura (freshwater crayfish), and other small fishes called bullies (cockabullies). The liberated trout thrived and by 1910 fish weighing 9 kg were being caught. In the early 1920s the food supply became so depleted that trout lost condition and the government introduced netting to reduce stocks. Then in 1934 the native smelt (*Retropinna retropinna*) was introduced from Rotorua as a food source. This proved to be very successful and smelt are now the main food supply for Taupo trout.

In 1926, thanks largely to the cooperation of the local Maori tribes, a law was passed entitling anglers holding a current Taupo fishing licence to free access along a 20 m strip around the shores of Lake Taupo and along the banks of most Taupo rivers.

Lake Taupo is the largest lake in New Zealand: 40 km long, 30 km wide and over 600 km^2. It has an average depth of 120 m (the deepest point is 160 m), and is 360 m above sea level.

This fishery fully deserves its worldwide reputation, as it offers a wide variety of superb angling water. Rainbow trout in Taupo are like steelhead in the North Pacific, in that they treat the lake like a sea. The average weight of trout caught varies between years, but is usually around 1.6 kg. Fish weighing over 4 kg are not uncommon, but most of these are browns. However, trophy rainbow are still caught. Most fish landed by fly anglers are caught on wet flies (known as lures or streamer flies) and nymphs, although there is some dry-fly fishing available in the surrounding streams. Boat fishing accounts for large numbers of fish.

The movement of trout in the lake follows the life cycle of smelt (small silvery fish), and the spawning run. Between April and September, 60 percent of trout in Lake Taupo run up the rivers and streams to spawn. Naturally, river and stream-mouth fishing are popular during these months. Fry that hatch and survive enter the lake 9–12 months later as fingerlings 15–20 cm long and reach maturity in two to four years. Post-spawning fish (known as kelts or slabs) return to the lake from October to December, about the same time that smelt school in the shallows and river mouths to spawn. Trout feed voraciously on these to regain condition and during these months shoreline smelt fishing and stream-mouth fishing are popular.

After January, shoreline fishing becomes unproductive but stream-mouth fishing, especially at night, remains good. From the end of May, when river temperatures equal lake temperatures, fish feed in the deeper waters of the lake and only enter stream mouths briefly before running up to spawn. Deep trolling then becomes an effective method.

Fish can still be caught during the winter months, but action tends to be slower in the lake, whereas river fishing comes into its own.

Fly fishing at stream and river mouths

Trout feed along the lip where the river delta drops off into deeper water, and along the edges of the current where it merges with the lake water. When fishing, it is important to stand back a few

Season and restrictions

➢ Lake Taupo is open all year. A separate Taupo licence is required.

Restrictions

Only the most important ones are listed here.

➢ Anglers must obtain a copy of the regulations from local sports stores or from DoC, and must be familiar with these when fishing Taupo. There is no excuse for ignorance!

➢ Fishing is prohibited between midnight and 5 am.

➢ No more than two lures or flies may be used at any one time.

➢ In fly-only waters, weighted flies must not be tied on a hook longer than 17 mm or deeper than 5.5 mm (about size 10). Bead heads are legal within the above size limitations.

➢ Strike indicators must be made from natural or synthetic yarn only. They can be dyed and impregnated with floatant.

➢ In fly-only waters it is illegal to use split shot, sinkers, weights, bubbles, fly spoons or artificial floats.

➢ Spinning is not permitted in any of the streams or rivers flowing into

metres from the lip as fish usually take the fly during the retrieve just as it passes over the lip. Wading is normally necessary and waders are essential to protect against the cold, especially at night or in the cooler months. Thigh waders may be sufficient at shallow river mouths, but chest waders are essential for deeper water.

At shallow mouths, false casting above the water is recommended as excessive water disturbance, even at night, frightens feeding fish. Most Taupo stream mouths can be fished with a medium-sinking or floating line. A weight-forward line will enable a longer cast, which is important when fishing pressure is high. Generally, a strong onshore wind makes fishing difficult, although at times when the current runs parallel to the shore the 'hot spot' may be 50 m along the beach. A light onshore breeze may be conducive to good fishing.

There is no substitute for experience, as each stream or river mouth has its own character. When the fishing is slow, a number

Lake Taupo, in the Tokaanu Tailrace above the main road bridge (SH 41) or within 300 m of any stream mouth.

- All bait fishing is prohibited. It is illegal to harl or troll within 300 m of any stream mouth, except for the Waikino and Otupotu Falls in the western bays.
- Boat owners must obtain a permit from local stores or tackle shops before using a public boat-launching ramp.
- Lead and wire lines are permitted. Downriggers are permitted but the cable must be no longer than 40 m and lines must be unweighted.
- Set rods on boats are legal only if every person on the boat is licensed.
- Fly fishing from an anchored boat is only permitted at the following stream mouths: Tongariro, Tauranga–Taupo, Waikino and Otupoto Falls. A float-tube or kick-boat is classed as a boat.
- The daily bag limit is three trout, and the minimum size is 450 mm.

Etiquette

We cannot stress too strongly that anglers fishing the Tongariro–Taupo Conservancy must understand the local etiquette (see Introduction, pp 20–21).

of options may be tried. Try changing position, but before doing so check with other anglers and do not force your way into a prime spot unless there is an obvious gap or you are joining the end of the line. Sometimes fish may not be feeding along the lip and it may be worth wading well out and casting into the tail of the current. Do not fish in front of another angler and, if in doubt, ask the others before making such a move.

Other tactics when the fishing is slow include changing lines and trying a dissimilar-sized fly or different fly patterns. Some flies do not swim well and set up unusual vibrations in the water. Altering the speed of your retrieve is another tactic worth trying. Sometimes fish simply stay out in deep water until very late. At night, if no fish have been caught by 9 pm, then it is worth spreading the 'bad news' to other anglers or even talking about how nice it would be in a warm bed. Many will agree and leave, and hopefully the fish will then come into the rip.

At small stream mouths, wading and false casting on the water may only drive feeding fish out further. It can also be beneficial periodically to 'spell' the mouth and allow spooked fish to return and begin feeding in close again. It may be difficult, however, to convince other anglers to cooperate with this type of suggestion.

Fishing is generally better on dark, moonless nights or when the barometer is rising after a front has passed. There are exceptions, however.

During the day, when fish are smelting through the rip, action can be fast and furious or totally frustrating. Trout can be seen gorging on smelt and, although many of these fish will be kelts, fishing is invariably fascinating. If trout are ignoring your fly, try a small pattern such as a size 12. When all else fails, a nymph fished along the edge of the current can bring results.

Flies for during the day

There are many successful lure patterns to use. During the day, try some of the older ones such as Grey Ghost, Green Smelt, Taupo Tiger, Jack Spratt or a Doll Fly. The more modern Mylar-bodied patterns can be deadly at times. When fish are feeding like crazy, even dropping your fly on the water in front of them may result in a strike. However, finding a good lure pattern when the fishing is tough is the real challenge.

Flies for night-time

At night, most black flies that swim well will take fish. These include Hairy Dog, Black Prince, Black Marabou, Craig's Night-time and Fuzzy Wuzzy in sizes 2–6. Use a stronger tippet with the larger sizes. Some anglers fish two flies, one with a luminous body. When all else fails, try a daytime smelt pattern.

Smelt fishing along the beaches

Walking the beaches on a hot, bright day searching for smelting fish is our favourite Taupo fishing. November and December are the best months. Wear shorts, sandshoes, hat, polarised sunglasses and sunscreen.

At times, schooling fish break the surface, throwing caution to the wind in their efforts to round up and feed on these tiny spawning fish. A quick cast and fast retrieve are required, using a floating line and a small smelt fly. In very calm, bright conditions, casting directly at fish frightens them. Try stalking with a slow-sinking line and only retrieving when a fish approaches. This is an exciting way to fish, especially in the company of another angler as one can spot for the other.

Fishing Taupo rivers

From the end of March to the end of November, the vast majority of Taupo trout intent on spawning enter the rivers and streams flowing into the lake. By July the rivers are full of fish. By September many will be spent and drifting back downstream to the lake to recover. A run of fish usually enters a river as a fresh (a rush or sudden flood of water in a creek or river) recedes and makes its way upstream over the next few days. The run may be spread over several kilometres of river and the rest of the river may be very quiet. Thirty days is the average length of time for a run of fish to reach the Whitikau tributary, about 15 km up the Tongariro River, although it can vary from 18 to 80 days. However, some fish even spawn in the main stream itself. Most hen fish are caught soon after they enter the river and are moving upstream, but jacks are more aggressive and will snap at a lure or nymph at any time. After a fresh, start in the lower reaches but during a period of fine weather, try further upstream. It is important to change location on the river if the fishing is poor.

Trout tend to lie in the deeper parts of pools or under banks where there is maximum cover and protection. The term 'lie' is frequently used when describing a pool, and means simply where trout lie or are expected to lie in the pool. When trout move up the river to spawn, they often run at night and rest during the day in a lie. This is usually a deep, slower-flowing, sheltered section of the pool where fish can conserve energy. Each pool has a favoured lie, and some have more than one. To be successful, an angler must cover the lie being fished, at the same depth that the trout are holding. Usually this means 'dredging' the bottom of the river. Trout will often move some distance sideways to intercept a lure or nymph fished at their depth but they seldom bother with lures that pass overhead.

Downstream lure fishing

In the smaller streams and rivers, a 6 or 7-weight rod and a reel holding a medium-sinking line of similar weight can be used, but in the larger Tongariro River an 8 or 9-weight rod and a high-density or shooting-head line should be used. A short tippet of 2–2.5 m with a breaking strain not less than 3.5 kg is suitable for the larger rivers, with a lighter tippet in the smaller streams. The lure should be cast across or even slightly upstream on a long cast, the line mended two or three times as the lure sinks and the lure retrieved through the lie. The 'take' usually occurs at the end of the swing and there is nothing so exciting as a fat, fresh-run rainbow smashing at the fly.

Subtle variations can be made with regard to casting, mending the line, covering each section of the pool and altering the speed of retrieve. Downstream lure fishing tends to be more successful on a fresh run of fish, and becomes harder during periods of low flow, clear water and bright sunny days. It pays to use smaller lures in these conditions.

Favoured lures in sizes 4–10 include Rabbit flies, Red Setter, Hairy Dog, Mrs Simpson, Mallard patterns and Woolly Buggers. Some anglers fish egg patterns on a sinking line. Many new patterns of lures are being produced, some with fluorescent bodies, but it is difficult to improve on the first two listed.

Upstream nymph fishing

The same weight of rod can be used to fish nymphs and lures, but with a floating line of corresponding weight. On the larger rivers where a long drift is important, we prefer a weight-forward floating line.

For the smaller streams, one weighted nymph can be used, with or without an indicator, but on the Tongariro River most anglers use two nymphs and an indicator. The nymph closer to you is often used simply as a weight, while the one at the end can be unweighted. It is unwise to use too heavy a rig, as it can be very unwieldy and difficult to cast – after a couple of blows to the back of the head from heavy nymphs you may be only too glad to go home. However, it is pointless drifting your nymphs a metre or so over the fish's head; they must sink well down through the lie. The total length of the trace should be 4–4.5m and the nymphs can be tied 30–50 cm apart. The strength of the trace will vary according to the water being fished, but generally a simple knotless length of 2.5–4 kg nylon is preferred.

An indicator of wool or synthetic yarn soaked in floatant is usually tied to the first metre of leader by a simple overhand knot.

The depth of water being fished determines the distance from the indicator to the nymphs. As a general rule, it should be one and a half times the depth. However, if the nymphs are not touching the bottom of the river then the distance can be increased. To help the leader sink, some anglers reduce the surface tension by washing it in soap solution or detergent, or running it through sand or Fuller's earth.

A long cast upstream with a long drift is very important in the Tongariro River, as this ensures your nymphs have plenty of time to sink and drift deeply through the lie. Allow the nymphs to float down naturally, as drag will cause them to rise. Although contact should be maintained with the nymphs, some slack line can be an advantage, as a perfectly straight line cast will be affected by drag. The indicator should be watched closely and any unusual movement such as sinking, deviating or slowing should immediately be acted on by striking. All water can be explored with nymphs, and pocket water should not be neglected. If you are the first angler on a pool at dawn, the fish may well be sitting in shallow water, so fish the edges first.

Favoured nymphs include Hare and Copper, Halfback, Pheasant Tail, White Caddis and Bug Eye. Egg patterns include a variety of Muppet and Glow Bug creations. The most common and successful rig for the Tongariro River is a combination of well weighted Bug Eye or Bead Head with an unweighted egg pattern.

Favoured locations round Lake Taupo

Trout can be caught anywhere in Lake Taupo. Stream mouths are top locations, but many rocky points around the lake also provide good fishing. Trout tend to cruise the 'blue line' or drop-off, the junction between inshore shallows and deeper water. Before picking a location, make certain there is not a strong onshore wind.

STREAM AND RIVER MOUTHS

Eastern lakeshore

MANGAKURA STREAM: A small stream entering the lake 1 km north of the Waitahanui mouth. Well worth exploring when fish are smelting and at night. You are unlikely to be disturbed by other anglers.

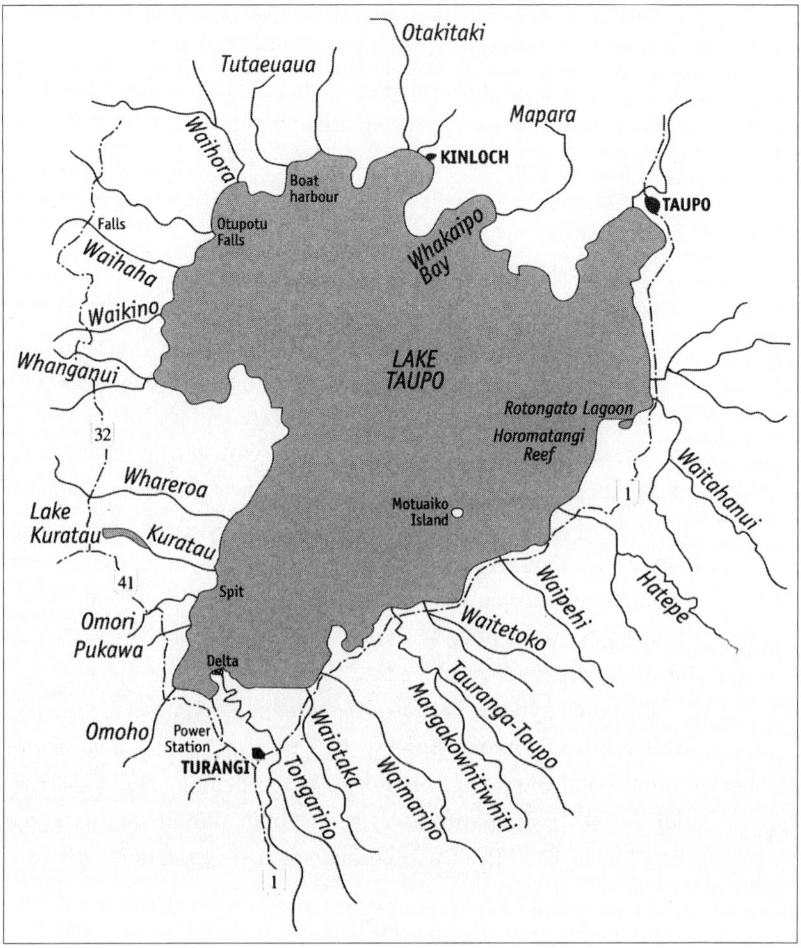

Lake Taupo

WAITAHANUI RIVER MOUTH: The most famous river mouth on Lake Taupo, not because of the number of fish caught but because of the 'picket fence' or line of anglers easily viewed from the main highway. This is not the place for a beginner, as a long cast with a medium-sinking line is essential to compete with other anglers. After a westerly storm, the current will be forced along the beach and 200 m of the rip can be fished without wading. The mouth is also well known as a place to catch trophy brown trout, usually at night during February and March.

OTUPATA CREEK: Drains the Rotongaio Lagoon. There is good smelt fishing south along the beach at the foot of the White Cliffs all the way to Hatepe. The mouth is worth trying at night.

HATEPE RIVER MOUTH: When other rivers run dirty after rain, try this mouth, which often remains clear as it drains two small hydro lakes. You can drive to the mouth, which is a favourite spot when fish are running.

WAITETOKO STREAM MOUTH: Very small stream with a shallow mouth entering Manowharangi Bay. Suits a floating line at night.

TAURANGA–TAUPO RIVER MOUTH: Before wading and fishing this mouth at night, anglers are strongly advised to inspect it during the day. It is very deep and can be dangerous for wading, but there is good fishing off the spit. Many anglers fish it from an anchored boat positioned so they can cast over the deep lip with a fast-sinking line. Fishing can be excellent, especially at night.

WAIPEHI STREAM MOUTH: There is a delightful rest area beneath the kowhai trees at this small stream mouth. It is very shallow and rocky but trout often come in very close at night so deep wading is unnecessary. Fishes well all year. Use a floating line.

WAIMARINO RIVER MOUTH: There is a rough track off SH 1 just south of the Waimarino bridge to the mouth. Then walk north along the beach. The drop-off can be fished only when the lake is low, as a long wade out may be needed to reach it. At this point the current is barely perceptible and a few changes of position may be necessary to find the 'hot spot'. Use a fast or medium-sinking line, cast over the lip and wait a few minutes before retrieving. If the lake level is above normal, carry a landing net, otherwise fish will need to be beached 100 m behind you. Fishes well all year but beware of a strong northeaster. Some anglers fish this mouth with large Glow Bugs using the 'heave-and-leave' method, while others have success fishing Booby flies on shooting-head lines.

Southern lakeshore

WAIOTAKA STREAM MOUTH: Turn off SH 1 onto Frethey's Road and the yacht club carpark and walk south along the beach to the mouth. This medium-sized stream has a shallow mouth best fished with a floating line. It has a reputation for large browns that feed at night, especially after heavy rain, on tadpoles and frogs washed out of the surrounding swamp. This mouth can be 'hot' at times.

TONGARIRO RIVER MOUTH: The delta is a prime fishing spot, but can only be reached by boat. The severe floods of 1998 changed the main mouth. Choosing which mouth to fish depends on the wind direction. The boat should be anchored with the transom barely hanging over the lip. Using a fast-sinking or high-density line, cast out as far as possible over the lip and wait a few minutes before retrieving. Be very careful if you decide to go ashore, as wading along the deep soft pumice lip can be dangerous. In favourable conditions, fishing at the delta can be quite superb.

TOKAANU TAILRACE: From November to February, when smelt are running, the screens at the Tokaanu powerhouse impede their upstream progress. Schools of these tiny fish gather in confusion and are easy prey to marauding trout. At times, good fly fishing can be had from the banks of the tailrace, especially upstream of the main road bridge. Weed can cause difficulties at times but the tailrace has a reputation for large trout. Fish can also be caught at the mouth of the tailrace and from the Tokaanu wharf, close by. Note that fishing is not permitted between the powerhouse and a marker located approximately 110 m downstream. Spinning is only permitted below the SH 41 bridge.

TOKAANU, SLIP (OMOHO), OMORI, PUKAWA STREAM MOUTHS: All can be reached from SH 41 between Tokaanu and Kuratau, and should be fished at night with floating lines. False casting is recommended and there is room for only two or three rods at each mouth. Little wading is needed. Most are productive all year. Fishing in the streams is prohibited. Explore these stream mouths during the day before stumbling around in the dark unaware of stream direction, depth of water and location of the lip.

KURATAU RIVER MOUTH: This shallow delta is safe to wade and excellent fishing can be experienced when trout are smelting. Use a floating line both during the day and at night. The Kuratau Spit, a few hundred metres south of the mouth, is also well worth fishing as the lip runs close inshore.

WHAREROA STREAM MOUTH: Can be reached by car from the Kuratau hydro road, off SH 32. This is another relatively shallow mouth which, along with the beach, fishes well during the smelting season. It also has a reputation for large browns which can be caught at night, sometimes as far as 50 m south of the mouth, especially when the current parallels the shore.

Western lakeshore

WHANGANUI STREAM MOUTH: This is generally reached by boat. A rough private road through Whakarawa Block on SH 32 is unreliable and has been completely washed out at times, becoming impassable even to 4WDs. Over the past few years, especially when the lake level is low, boats have been unable to shelter in the river mouth. It is almost 20 km from the nearest boat ramp at either Kinloch or Kuratau. During the smelting season there is very good stream mouth and beach fishing. Use either a floating or slow-sinking line. If action is slow at the rip, try either end of the beach. There is good night fishing as well at the mouth, but like all mouths it can, at times, be quite dead. The Whanganui Stream is open to fishing 1 December–31 May. A long wade upstream or a scramble through scrub takes you to a pool below falls. There are usually a few fish here, although casting against the downdraft created by the falls can be taxing.

WAIKINO STREAM MOUTH: This stream gushes out of a rocky cleft between Whanganui and Waihaha bays, and can be reached only by boat. There is a peg in the rock on the north side of the current where a boat can be tied up. Use a high-density line to reach fish clearly seen feeding deep in the current. At times, night fishing can be hot, even off the rocky shelf to the south, but it is a long way from home if the wind gets up.

WAIHAHA RIVER MOUTH: Access is generally by boat; the nearest boat ramp is Kinloch. The bay can also be reached by walking down a steep track through bush from the end of Waihaha Road off SH 32. Although this mouth changes frequently during storms, it is usually deep enough to shelter a boat. Private camping can also be arranged with the owners. Fishing is best when the river current flows in the direction of Whakatonga (Richwhite) Point. During smelting, there is good beach and river-mouth fishing and also interesting fishing off the point itself. It is useful if a friend sits up high on the point and spots for you. The river is navigable for small boats up as far as Tieke Falls, and there are usually a few fish in the falls pool. The season for the river is 1 December–31 May.

OTUPOTO FALLS: Enter the lake at the south end of Waihora Bay. The usual method of fishing is trolling through the current, but flycasting from a boat is also popular.

WAIHORA RIVER MOUTH: Access is by boat from Kinloch but there is an excellent sheltered harbour close by in Boat Harbour at Kawakawa Point. There is good night fishing at this mouth and fish cruise and smelt along the beach in November and December. There are often a few large browns lying deep in the lower reaches of the river, but these are very wary and difficult to catch.

TUTAEUAUA (CHINAMANS) STREAM: This small stream enters the southern end of Kawakawa Bay. Access is generally by boat, but there is a private 4WD track off Whangamata Road to the cliff top. From there a walking track leads down through the bush to the beach. The stream mouth is 10 minutes' walk along the beach to the north. Usual methods apply to this shallow mouth including false casting, resting the water periodically, and fishing with a floating line. Wading is not usually necessary. Holds two rods comfortably and fishes best at night.

Northern lakeshore

OTAKETAKE STREAM MOUTH: This tiny stream can be reached only when the lake is low, by wading round a rocky point at the western end of Whangamata Bay.

WHANGAMATA STREAM MOUTH: Reached by walking west along the beach from Kinloch. Fish with a floating line at night.

MAPARA STREAM MOUTH: This small stream enters the eastern end of Whakaipo Bay. The mouth is very popular and heavily fished, especially at night. A strong southerly or westerly wind will make it unfishable. Use a floating or sink-tip line and the usual night lures. The eastern shoreline of Whakaipo Bay, south of the Mapara mouth, also fishes well when trout are smelting.

Trolling and harling Lake Taupo

More trout are taken from Lake Taupo by fishing from boats than by any other method. Small boats can be launched from most beaches. There are public boat ramps for larger craft on the Waikato River outlet, Acacia Bay, Kinloch, Kuratau Spit, Waihi, Tokaanu Wharf, Motuoapa and at Four Mile Bay or Wharewaka. Permits are required to use these ramps; and check the regulations (see pp 58–59).

In Maori the lake is sometimes called Taupo-hau-rau ('lake of a hundred winds') because of the strong southerly that can spring up unexpectedly. A short, steep chop of 1.5 m can be very troublesome, even for a 5 m boat with a 60 hp motor. Anglers are strongly advised to have the same safety equipment they would carry if fishing offshore at sea.

The VHF radio network for Taupo operates on channels 6, 8 and 61. Weather forecasts provided by the coastguard are broadcast at 0915, 1215, 1615 and 2015. Cellphones can also be useful.

Trout can be caught anywhere, even in the middle, but favoured trolling locations include Whanganui Bay, Kawakawa Bay, Mine Bay, Whangamata Bay, Whakaipo Reef, Rangatira Point, the Horomatangi Reef off Rotongaio, and off the Waitahanui River mouth (but remember not closer than 300 m from the river mouth).

When trout are smelting near the surface, from September to February, harling a smelt fly on a fly rod rigged with a high-density line can be very effective. Boat speed must be kept to a minimum, either by using a small auxiliary outboard motor or by slowing the boat with a sea-anchor. Let out the whole fly line and 20 m of backing so the fly sinks sufficiently. The trace should be 5–6 m long. Following the blue line or drop-off is recommended.

Flies to use include Parson's Glory, Ginger Mick, Orange, Yellow or Green Rabbit, Taupo Tiger, Grey Ghost, Green and Yellow Orbit in sizes 4–6.

In the autumn and winter, trout feed in much deeper water and wire and lead lines and downriggers come into their own. The wire line will sink deeper than either the lead line or the downrigger, which is restricted to 40 m, but has a nasty tendency to tangle. The downrigger provides more sport, as once a fish is hooked and breaks clear of the downrigger it can be played on a light unweighted monofilament line. Fish hooked on a wire line often initially feel like a piece of weed. Many variations can be tried; some anglers use a colour or two of lead line incorporated into their monofilament line. If using monofilament it pays to use 8 kg strength and let out 80–100 m. Do not turn the boat too sharply when trolling and be aware of other boats in the vicinity. When you catch a fish, turn and troll back through the same area. Do not forget to take a landing net!

Spinners to try include Toby and Cobra variations, Flatfish and Zed spinners of different colours and sizes.

Flowing into Lake Taupo

WAITAHANUI RIVER

☐ Location

Rises from springs in the northern end of the Kaimanawa Forest Park and flows generally west to enter Lake Taupo a few kilometres south of the town of Taupo.

☐ Access

The lower reaches are accessed from SH 1 on either side of the main road bridge. The mouth is reached from a walking track off SH 1 north of the Waitahanui bridge.

Access to the upper river pools is from Blake Road, which leaves SH 1 south of the Waitahanui Bridge. There are walking tracks along the banks.

The middle reaches are accessed from Mill Road, off SH 1.

The headwaters are reached from forestry roads behind Iwitahi on SH 5, and permission is required from Forestry New Zealand – but it is hardly worth the trouble as the river is deep, overgrown and impossible to fish.

☐ Season and restrictions

Above the Te Arero Stream confluence, 1 December–31 May. Below the Te Arero Stream confluence the main river is open all year. For the Mangamutu tributary, which joins the Waitahanui immediately above the main road bridge, the season is 1 December–31 May.

Because this medium-sized river is spring-fed, it seldom discolours after rain. The riverbed is rock, stone and fine pumice, and above the middle reaches the banks are scrub-covered. Below the Waitahanui bridge fishing pressure is usually very intense, especially after fresh-run fish have entered the river. Most anglers fish this section with a fast-sinking line and lure, though some nymph-fish the pools on either side of the bridge. In bright conditions when the water is clear, fish can be spotted in some sections. Around Easter and after a good southerly storm, many fish can be seen under the main road bridge.

The middle and upper pools offer a different challenge. While there is 7 km of river to fish and some pools are relatively straightforward, others are overgrown by scrub and are very awkward to fish. The river is swift in parts but there are some excellent deep holding pools. Downstream lure fishing with a high-density line and upstream nymphing methods are equally popular. The river can be waded but some runs are deep and swift, and care should be taken. Angling pressure is much less in these reaches of river and the environment is very tranquil and pleasant. The usual lures and nymphs, as described under Fishing Taupo Rivers (see pp 61–62), can be used. Our favourite lure is a size 4–6 Orange Rabbit.

HINEMAIAIA (HATEPE) RIVER

☐ Location

Drains the western boundary of the Kaimanawa Forest Park between the Waitahanui and Waipehi watersheds; it flows northwest and enters Lake Taupo at the village of Hatepe on SH 1. The headwaters and upper reaches have been severely modified for hydroelectric power generation and are not worth exploring.

☐ Access

An access track to the middle reaches runs upstream on the true left bank off SH 1 on the south side of the Hatepe Bridge. This takes you to the limit of fishing 300 m below the dam, marked by a sign. The lower river is reached downstream from the SH 1 bridge or upstream from the mouth.

☐ Season and restrictions

Above the main road bridge, 1 December–31 May. Below this bridge the river is open all year.

Above the bridge, this small stream has some moderately deep holes and good lies against the banks, although in places overhanging vegetation can impede casting. Hooked fish have every chance of escaping by diving under sunken logs and tangling round snags. Fluctuations in water flow from hydroelectric power generation have caused bank erosion and deterioration in recent years. However, at times there is still good nymph and downstream lure fishing. Some trout can be spotted but many lie hidden under the banks.

Below the bridge, the water is better suited to downstream lure fishing. Rollcast or float your line downstream and retrieve slowly and deeply against the banks.

TAURANGA–TAUPO RIVER

☐ Location

Rises in the Kaimanawa Forest Park, flows northwest, initially through native bush, then exotic forest and lastly, pastoral land to enter Lake Taupo near Te Rangiita.

☐ Access

HEADWATERS: From Kiko Road, which leaves SH 1 south of the main road bridge over the Tauranga–Taupo River. As there is usually a locked gate on Kiko Road a lot of walking is required to fish this section of river; or use a mountain bike.

UPPER REACHES: The river can be explored from the Ranger's Pool simply by walking upstream and into a gorge.

MIDDLE REACHES ABOVE SH 1 BRIDGE: After two severe floods, vehicle access is now permitted on Tuki Road on the south side of the SH 1 bridge only. There is a designated carpark and a few confusing walking tracks upstream from this point. Keeping to the river or following the old dry riverbed may be the best option for anglers who wish to reach the Cliff Pool. It is not clear, at the time of writing, what measures Environment Waikato will eventually take to stabilise the river between SH 1 and the Cliff Pool. It is now a long walk (50 mins) to the Ranger's Pool.

LOWER REACHES AND MOUTH: From a side road just south of the main road bridge.

☐ Season and restrictions

Above the Ranger's Pool and the Mangakowhitiwhiti Stream, 1 December–31 May. Below the Mangakowhitiwhiti Stream the river is open for fishing all year.

This medium-sized river was severely affected by the 1998 floods, when the river simply cut through and isolated the well known Crescent Pool, which is now almost dry. Then, in December 2001

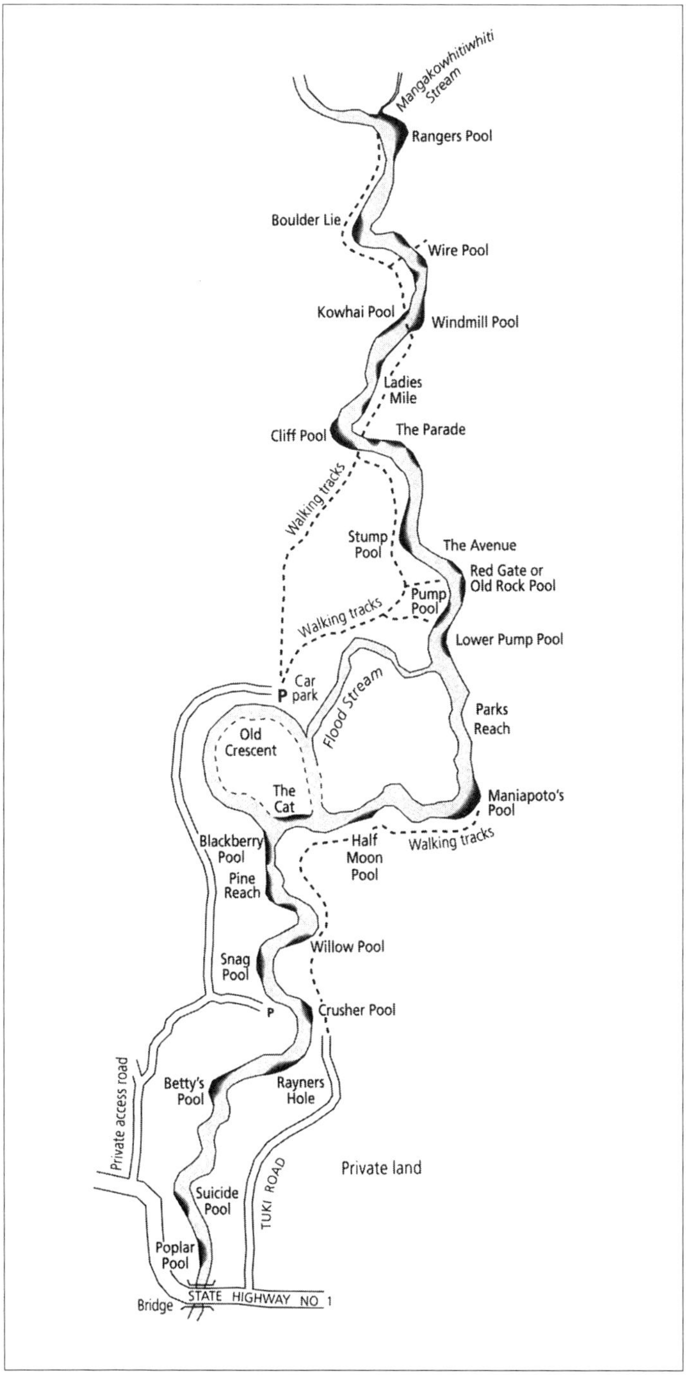
Mangakowhitiwhiti Stream
Rangers Pool
Boulder Lie
Wire Pool
Kowhai Pool
Windmill Pool
Ladies Mile
Cliff Pool
The Parade
Walking tracks
Stump Pool
The Avenue
Red Gate or Old Rock Pool
Pump Pool
Walking tracks
Lower Pump Pool
P Car park
Flood Stream
Old Crescent
Parks Reach
The Cat
Maniapoto's Pool
Blackberry Pool
Half Moon Pool
Walking tracks
Pine Reach
Willow Pool
Snag Pool
P
Crusher Pool
Private access road
Betty's Pool
Rayners Hole
Private land
TUKI ROAD
Suicide Pool
Poplar Pool
Bridge
STATE HIGHWAY NO 1

Tauranga-Taupo River

in another massive flood, the river breached its banks at the Cliff Pool, cut through to the quarry and partially restored the Crescent. Most of the other pools changed but have remained more or less in their old locations. Fish can be caught throughout the whole river, right up to the falls in the headwaters.

The upper reaches and headwaters should be fished in summer after 1 December. There is sight fishing for both recovering and resident rainbows but you need to be reasonably fit to fish this section. Trout will take dry flies and nymphs but a lot of scrambling and walking is required to negotiate some sections of the gorge. Once in the gorge, it is difficult to climb out.

By far the most popular and heavily fished section is the middle reaches. A few resident fish remain after the spawning runs but the time to fish this river is between the end of March and the end of September, and preferably after a fresh. With luck, the river will be full of fighting fresh-run rainbows and the fishing can be thrilling. Although some fish can be spotted, the majority hide under banks, logs and riffles or lie deep in pools.

This is an easy river to fish as crossings can usually be made without difficulty and wading is safe. The banks are mostly clear for casting, so all sections of water can be covered. Fish are caught equally on nymphs and lures although lure fishing becomes hard when the river is low and clear. Be sure to fish to the trout that lie under banks of blackberry: they will take both lures and nymphs. At times, this river seems almost barren of fish but after a shower or two of rain the action returns.

The lies are not difficult to recognise. In the deeper pools, the lie is usually toward the tail of the pool where there is less current. Most fish can be beached on the shingle toward the tail of runs and pools, so a landing net is not required. There is a good two days' fishing on this river up to the Ranger's Pool, but you will seldom have it all to yourself.

WAIMARINO RIVER

☐ Location

Drains the western boundary of the Kaimanawa Forest Park, then flows northwest by Korohe Pa to enter Lake Taupo north of Turangi.

☐ Access

UPPER REACHES: Unless a friend drops you off at Korohe Pa from Korohe Road, there is a lot of walking, as parking your vehicle on SH 1 is recommended.

MIDDLE REACHES: This stretch of water lies between SH 1 and Korohe Pa. SH 1 crosses the river and a vehicle track leads up the true left bank for a short distance. The top section is reached from Korohe Road, which leads to Korohe Crossing.

LOWER REACHES: These can be accessed from SH 1 bridge or from the mouth. A vehicle track runs from SH 1 down the true left (southern) bank, albeit some distance from the river, and you can then walk north along the lakeshore to the mouth.

☐ Season and restrictions

Above Korohe Crossing, 1 December–31 May. Below this point the river is open all year.

In the upper reaches of this small river, trout can run up to the falls in the vicinity of Te Pahatu trig. There are usually a few resident trout, but early in the season most fish will be recovering spawners. There are some delightful pools and runs for anglers prepared to walk and scramble. The banks of scrub, native bush and exotic forest do not impede casting, although drag can be a problem when fishing short pools. Fish can be spotted in this river, which is easily crossed.

In the middle reaches there are a few pools upstream from SH 1 that hold run fish, especially after a fresh. These are easily sighted and can be taken on nymphs, especially early in the day. Also try fishing a downstream lure under the banks of toetoe, scrub and grass. It is hard to beat a Red Setter or Orange Rabbit, but if the river is high or slightly discoloured, try a green-bodied lure.

The lower reaches are more overgrown and there is less holding water, but after rain, fish can be taken on a well sunk lure fished downstream by rollcasting.

WAIOTAKA STREAM

□ Location

Lies south of the Waimarino and runs parallel to it.

□ Access

The upper reaches running through Hautu Prison farm are now closed to anglers. The middle reaches can be accessed from SH 1 by two signposted access tracks and from the first road right north of the Tongariro River bridge out of Turangi. Drive past Hautu Prison to the Hautu Ford. A walking track follows from the ford downstream on the true left bank.

□ Season and restrictions

Above Hautu Ford (a marker 100 m upstream), 1 December–31 May. Below this marker the stream is open all year.

Although this small to medium-sized stream is fast flowing and overgrown by scrub in parts, there is good fishing for run fish, especially after rain. The pool immediately above the ford is very popular with guides and beginners as there is every chance of catching a fish. There is not a lot of holding water but fish sheltering in deep water under banks can be tempted by a lure fished downstream. Nymphing is generally more difficult because scrub along the banks may prevent an accurate cast and a good long drift. It is wise to carry a landing net as a hooked fish will turn and run downstream very rapidly. There are few spots where a fish can be easily beached and underwater snags present problems. It is generally not overcrowded by anglers.

TONGARIRO RIVER

□ Location

Drains the Kaimanawa Ranges by way of its major tributary, the Waipakihi River, and Lake Rotoaira by way of the Poutu River and canal. The upper reaches have been modified for hydroelectric power generation. The main river flows generally northwards, through the outskirts of Turangi, and enters Lake Taupo 10 km further north.

☐ **Access**

In July 1998, two major floods a week apart severely affected this world-famous river, changing many pools and washing out access tracks. Some of the tracks have been repaired but others may never be restored to their original condition.

UPPER REACHES (above the Fence Pool): Access upstream is difficult as there are few tracks through the bush and the river gorges. It is best to raft downstream from below the hydro dam. Access to the dam and Beggs Pool from SH 1 is by way of Access 10 and the Kaimanawa Road.

MIDDLE REACHES (between the Fence Pool and SH 1 bridge):

1. At the Poutu Bridge on SH 1 south of Turangi there is a rough vehicle track that now goes only as far as the Break-away carpark. Pools upstream from this point can only be reached by walking. A branch off this track to the left leads to the reformed Dreadnought Pool. Take care when turning out of this track back onto the main highway, as visibility is poor.
2. A walking access track off SH 1 about 100 m south of the Red Hut carpark leads to both of the Waddell's Pools.
3. Red Hut carpark, signposted. A swingbridge crosses the river to access tracks that lead both up and downstream on the true right bank.
4. Duchess Pool, signposted. Walking access track off SH 1.
5. Tongariro National Trout Centre. Gate closing times are marked but you can park either inside at the carpark or outside the gate. Tracks lead to Barlow's, Birch, Silly and Duchess pools on the true left bank.
6. Admiral's Pool Road, signposted off SH 1 leads to Kamahi, the new Admiral's Pool and the Stag on the true left bank.
7. Kutai Street, off Taupehi Road, leads to the Hydro Pool.
8. The access to the Major Jones carpark, footbridge and pool is signposted from Taupehi Road. It is prudent to lock your car and leave nothing valuable inside. Tracks run up and down the river from this footbridge.
9. Arahori Road, off Taupehi Road, leads to the Island Pool.
10. Te Aho Road, off Taupehi Road, leads to Judge's Pool.

LOWER REACHES (downstream from the main road bridge):

1. An access track leads downstream on the true left bank immediately below the main road bridge. There is a marked access track on the true right bank from the end of Herekiekie Street, which runs off Graces Road north of the bridge.
2. A vehicle track from Tautahanga Road at the back of Turangi township leads to the true left bank. This has been severely damaged by floods and is washed out below Bain Pool. Foot access is now possible only below this.
3. Bain Pool carpark on the right bank can be reached from Graces Road. The track downstream to the Reed Pool has been damaged but will probably be reformed by anglers walking downstream.
4. Access further downstream on the true left bank via Hirangi and Awamate roads has been severely affected, with the lower end of Awamate Road still under water. There is still foot access, however, for anglers prepared for a long walk.

☐ Season and restrictions

Above the Fence Pool, 1 December–31 May.
Below the Fence Pool, the river is open for fishing all year.

It is wise to be acutely aware of etiquette before fishing the Tongariro River (see pp 20–21). Angling pressure can be very heavy, and some anglers become very protective of 'their' stretch of water. It is important to move either downstream or upstream with every few casts and not hog one section.

The river can be crossed in a few places by fit, competent anglers but this is a large swift river and risks should be kept to a minimum. It is not an easy river for the novice as generally a long cast, often with well weighted nymphs, is required to cover the lies. However, trout use the main river for spawning as well as access to the tributaries. Although the important pools have been described, fish often lie elsewhere, such as in pocket water or close to the banks, especially early in the morning. Try some unusual spots away from other anglers.

The middle reaches upstream from the SH 1 bridge are more picturesque, with patches of manuka scrub and native bush growing along the banks. Below this bridge the river is more open, with gravel banks lined by willows.

In summer, when angling pressure is minimal, good dry-fly fishing can be had. The Major Jones Pool has a reputation for summer fishing. Try an Elk Hair Caddis or a soft-hackle wet fly towards evening. Large browns also enter the lower river in January. These will accept dry flies during the day or a well sunk green Woolly Bugger fished across and downstream.

This world-famous river still deserves its reputation. Trout average a little less than 2 kg, but there is the possibility of a trophy fish. There is no better place than the Tongariro River when the action is hot; but during spells of dry, sunny weather the fishing becomes very slow and tedious.

Tongariro pools

The naming of the Tongariro River pools is steeped in history and, although some of the original pools have gone, others close to the original location have been given the old name. Some new pools formed have been given the title of 'upper' or 'lower' depending on their location and with reference to the original pool.

Major floods in July 1998 so changed this large river that some anglers who had fished it for years virtually gave up in disgust. These were the third and fourth-largest floods on record. The Whitikau, Boulder and Fan Pools were destroyed and even the boulder itself disappeared from the Boulder Pool. However, new pools formed and much of the silt and ash from the Mt Ruapehu eruptions was flushed out of the river. The Dreadnought Pool, famous in Zane Grey's time, has reformed.

The following is a brief outline of the main pools and the changes that have occurred.

Middle reaches

FENCE POOL: It is a 25-minute walk upstream from the Breakaway carpark to this pool, which has been fishing well from the true left bank. There is a lie on the true right toward the tail of the pool that can be nymph-fished, but the river crossing can be difficult.

SAND POOL: This pool has remained unscathed and is still deep and swirly and awkward to get a good drift. It is best fished from the true left bank. The tail of the pool can be crossed in low water by tall anglers, but now that the Whitikau Pool has gone there is no great advantage to be gained.

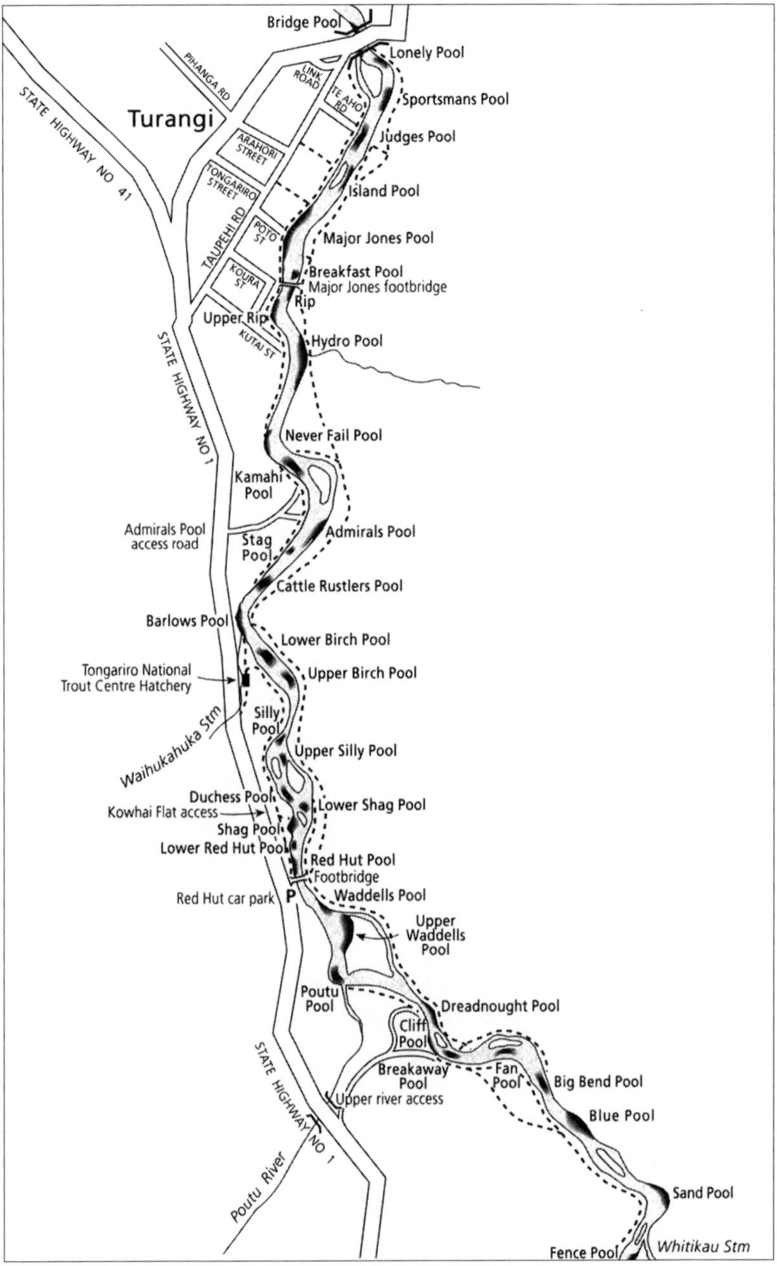

Middle Tongariro River

BLUE POOL: This very large, long, deep and stable pool is still fishing well, although it has changed. The lie runs the length of the pool and is over against the cliff. The middle section is difficult to wade, as there is deep water on the outside of a large log. No longer can an angler wade down the centre of the pool and fish. A long cast is still required to cover the lie, with the lower section the easiest. It is a 20-minute walk from the Breakaway carpark.

BIG BEND POOL: This pool lies well above the bend and offers good fishing from both sides of the river. The lie on the true right side is toward the tail but it is a 35-minute walk up river to this pool from the Red Hut swingbridge.

FAN POOL: The old Fan Pool has disappeared and been replaced by a pool further upstream. On the true left, a swift sidestream needs to be crossed before fishing but the pool looks promising.

BREAKAWAY POOL: This pool has suffered from the floods and does not hold the numbers of fish that it previously did. However, there is a good lie toward the tail on the right bank, and the left bank still fishes reasonably well. Angling pressure is now much less.

CLIFF POOL: This pool has entirely changed and now runs hard against the cliff on the left bank. It is deep and smooth and slow-flowing toward the tail. It can only be fished from the right. This entails a 20-minute walk upriver from the Red Hut bridge and crossing a small side creek.

DREADNOUGHT POOL: The original pool lay just upstream from the Poutu confluence. The new pool lies further upstream and is fishing very well, especially from the left bank. The right bank is covered with bush and scrub. You can drive to this pool with a 4WD vehicle by taking the left branch of the Breakaway access track at the Poutu bridge. It has become very popular because of the easy access and good-looking water.

POUTU POOL: This pool still lies against the cliff at the mouth of the Poutu River. It is a deep, stable pool and can be accessed by crossing the Red Hut swingbridge and walking upstream.

UPPER WADDELL'S POOL: This new pool is best fished from the left bank and is yielding some good bags of fish. It is an easy pool to fish and, in our opinion, will become very popular.

WADDELL'S POOL: Runs against a cliff on the right bank and can be fished only from the left bank. There is a foot access track to both Waddell's pools off SH 1 about 100 m south of the Red Hut carpark.

RED HUT POOL: This pool has changed considerably but still fishes well from the right bank. Cross the swingbridge from the Red Hut carpark and walk down to the river.

LOWER RED HUT POOL: This rather small new pool formed just downstream from the Red Hut Pool is also promising and recently yielded a beautiful 3.5 kg rainbow hen to a visiting angler. It fishes well from the right bank.

SHAG POOL: This is still deep and swirly and not easy to get a good drift. Walk downstream from the Red Hut swingbridge and fish it from the right bank.

UNNAMED POOL (UPPER DUCHESS): This new, promising pool is best fished from the left bank. The lower reaches on the right can also be nymph-fished until deep water runs against a cliff. Access to the right is difficult, as you need to drop down steeply through bush. Walk upstream from the Duchess Pool to fish the left bank.

DUCHESS POOL: This has completely changed and is now swifter and shallower than before. It can be fished from either bank. At present the easiest access to the left bank is by walking upstream from the National Trout Centre.

SILLY POOL: This pool has improved with the flood and can be fished from both sides, although a cliff restricts fishing on the right side midway up the pool.

BIRCH POOLS: These have virtually joined up since the flood and are not easily defined. Best fished from the left although the tail can be nymph-fished from the right. Access from the Trout Centre.

BARLOW'S POOL: Can now be fished from either bank, although a cliff on the left restricts fishing in the lower section. The left bank is accessed from the Trout Centre; the right bank by walking 20 minutes upstream from the Major Jones swingbridge or about 20 minutes downstream from the Red Hut swingbridge.

CATTLE RUSTLERS POOL: This pool has changed significantly. It fishes best from the right bank but some nymphing is also possible from the left.

ADMIRAL'S POOL: This has changed location and now lies further upstream. Best waded and fished from the left bank to a lie against the right bank. You can drive in on Admiral's Pool Road.

KAMAHI POOL: This pool is now good from both banks. Access to the left bank is from Admiral's Pool Road. The right bank can be fished by walking upstream from the Major Jones swingbridge.

NEVERFAIL POOL: This small pool should be fished from the right as it runs against a cliff. Cross the Major Jones swingbridge and walk upstream. There is a branch off the main track to the pool.

HYDRO POOL: This is still a very productive pool, especially for large browns, but the left side has filled in with stones and has become shallower. Wading is now easier from the left bank and the lie against the right bank can easily be covered with a good cast. Fish are still taken from various high perches along the right bank. Access from Kutai Street or by walking upstream from the Major Jones swingbridge on the right bank. Angling pressure is generally high. It pays to fish at dawn for trophy browns.

MAJOR JONES POOL: This long, deep, stable pool is still the largest on the river and, although some changes have occurred, the fishing is very much the same as before the floods. A long cast is still required from the right bank to satisfactorily cover the lies. The tail can still be nymph-fished although the lies have changed.

ISLAND POOL: This pool has improved and is fished from the left bank after crossing the sidestream, which also holds fish.

JUDGES POOL: This long pool offers excellent water from both banks although lure fishing is best from the right side. It is a long pool which slows and shallows out toward the tail, where it can be crossed in low water. Nymphing is good from the left bank, with access from Te Aho Road. Walk downstream for 15 minutes from the Major Jones swingbridge to fish the right bank. There is a side track through a small creek on the left.

SPORTSMAN'S POOL: This is still fished from the left bank. Walk downstream from Judges Pool.

LONELY POOL: Although this pool changed a couple of years before the 1998 floods, it remains in its new location against the cliff. It fishes best from the left by walking down from Judges or up from the main road bridge. Scrub on the backcast can be a nuisance.

Lower reaches

BRIDGE POOL: This is now smaller and extends upstream under the SH 1 bridge. Access to the left bank is from a track at the carpark. Access to the right bank is from the Herekiekie Street track or through scrub by the bridge.

LOWER BRIDGE POOL: This excellent popular new pool is heavily fished and easily observed downstream from the main road bridge. Access on the left is from the track at the carpark and on the right from the Herekiekie Street track. Best fished from the left bank.

SWIRL POOL: Has also changed since the floods and become long and narrow. Best from the right bank.

THE STONES POOL: This is now a small pool near the stopbank, and not very productive.

UPPER ISLAND POOL: This has also changed and is best fished from the left bank, as the lie runs on the right side of the pool. Access from the track off Tautahanga Road after wading through a small sidestream.

BAIN POOL: This large, deep pool is best fished from the right, although a willow stump is a bother on the backcast when fishing a lure downstream. Access is from a carpark down a shingle road off Graces Road.

The 1998 floods were so severe that the pools below this point lost definition and the river has become somewhat featureless, snag-infested and slow-flowing. The stony riverbed is now silt-covered, the banks show evidence of being under water and the walking tracks have been obliterated. Many of the willows have either died or been swept into the river. Some stretches are so snag-infested that a fly shop on the bank would make a handsome profit. The vehicle track is washed out beyond Bain Pool so the left bank downstream from here is accessible only on foot.

SHAW REACH: If you can identify this reach it is best fished from the left.

LOG POOL: This is one of the better lower-river pools, with enough definition to determine where it begins and where it ends. It can only be fished from the left because of trees along the right bank. Walk down through the willows from Bain Pool.

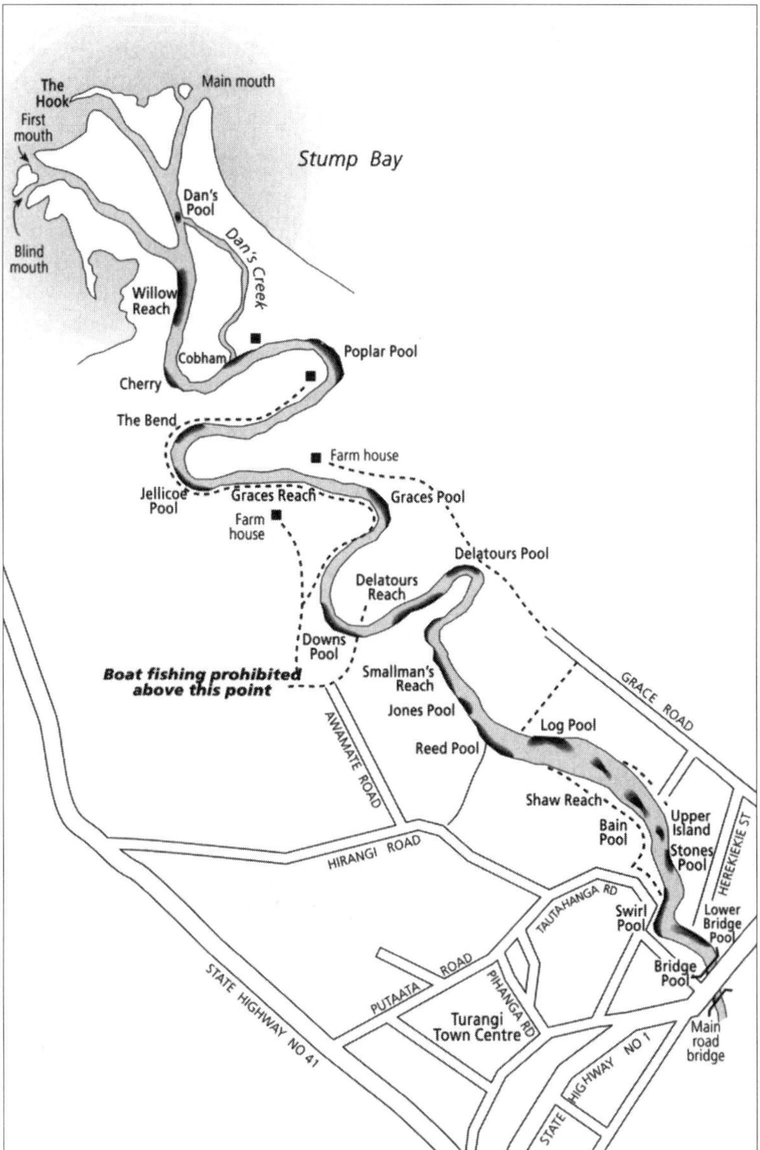

Lower Tongariro River

REED POOL: It is very difficult to determine where the lies are now located in this once very popular and productive pool. It can still be nymph-fished from the left bank as before, but fishing is best from the right. However, snags are a major problem for lure anglers with a long cast, especially as most fish appear to hold close to the left bank.

Below the Reed Pool, the river is like a long canal and not worth describing in detail. The definition of its pools may well return in time but the floods have caused so much havoc that the lower end of Awamate Road is still under water and the farmhouse has been evacuated. Snags continue to be a problem all the way down to the Poplar Pool. When we last walked the river, no lies could be defined and we landed no fish. No doubt it will gradually improve, as it obviously has done in the past.

LAKE ROTOAIRA

☐ Location and access

SH 47 skirts part of the southern shore, where the Rotoaira Fishing Camp is located. Te Ponanga Saddle Road, from Turangi and SH 41, briefly passes the northern shore.

☐ Boat launching

From the Rotoaira Fishing Camp. Small boats can be launched at the Wairehu Canal.

☐ Season and restrictions

1 September–30 June. As the lake is privately owned, anglers must obtain an entry permit from the Rotoaira Fishing Camp in addition to a Taupo licence, and abide by the owners' regulations.

This moderate-sized natural lake has a swampy, difficult shoreline so nearly all the fishing is done from boats. Harling a fly, casting from a boat or trolling a spinner can all be productive as the stocks of rainbows are high. Best fished from April to June, when fish should be in good condition and average 1–2 kg. Hydro-electric development has not improved this fishery but there is still excellent sport at times. We suggest trying lures such as Red Setter, Rabbit patterns, Kilwell No 1, Hamill's Killer and Woolly Bugger.

Trout can also be taken at the mouth of Wairehu Canal or from the groynes at the Poutu end of the lake.

LAKE OTAMANGAKAU

☐ Location and access

Lies on the opposite side of Te Ponanga Saddle Road to Lake Rotoaira, off SH 47. Access roads are signposted Whanganui Intake, Te Whaiau Dam, Otamangakau Dam, Boat Ramp and Wairehu Control Gate. There are basic camping facilities and a boat ramp.

☐ Season and restrictions

1 October–30 June. The bag limit is one fish.

The 'Big O' is probably as well known to overseas anglers seeking a trophy fish as it is to locals. Diverting the headwaters of the Whanganui River in 1971 formed this shallow, fertile hydro lake. It is 150 ha in area and lies on an exposed tussock and scrub plain. The view of the mountains close by in the Tongariro National Park compensates for the rather stark environment. The lake is subject to fluctuating levels and although this does not affect the fishing to any great extent it hardly adds to its charm, as the shoreline can become muddy and slippery. When the lake level is high, shoreline access becomes more difficult.

The lake holds browns and rainbows averaging over 2.5 kg, and each year at least one fish of 6-7 kg is landed. There is a reasonable stock of fish in the lake and, because there is so much food, some of them survive to a ripe old age while continuing to grow. Some trout have been found to be eight years old and to have spawned five times. Food consists of mayflies, caddis, snails, midges, dragonflies and damsel flies and various terrestrials, especially cicadas. There are no smelt or bullies in this lake.

While the majority of fish are caught from boats or float-tubes there is some excellent shoreline fishing in summer for sighted trout. Wading is safe but there are some swampy areas. The lake level can affect the shoreline fishing but large browns cruise the channels between the weed beds and can be stalked on a bright sunny summer's day. On a hot windy day in late January or February, cicada fishing can be most exciting. When fly fishing from a boat or float-tube use a sinking line, a small nymph and a slow retrieve. It pays to carry at least 100 m of backing on your reel as we have seen at least one angler 'cleaned out' by a trophy rainbow.

Trolling accounts for some fish but weed growth in the warmer months becomes a problem. When fly fishing try the following nymphs: Black and Peacock, Hare and Copper, Pheasant Tail, Zug Bug, Damsel, Dragonfly and Halfback. Suggested lures include Woolly Bugger, Hamill's Killer, Mrs Simpson, Red Setter and Rabbit patterns. Although the majority of fish are taken sub-surface, they can be caught on dry flies such as Coch-y-bondhu, Royal Wulff and Adams.

This lake has a well earned reputation for trophy fish, but they are not easy to catch and success may take many hours of fishing.

East of Taupo

RANGITIKEI RIVER

☐ Location

The river drains the Middle and Island ranges of the Kaimanawa Forest Park and flows generally south to the Taihape–Napier Road and then to Mangaweka. From Mangaweka to Bulls the river flows southwest parallel to, but east of, SH 1 and eventually enters the Tasman Sea west of Palmerston North. This long river holds trout throughout its length but only the upper reaches, above Springvale Bridge, are considered to be top fishing locations.

☐ Access

1. A rigorous two-day tramp over Umukarikari to the Waipakahi Hut and Junction Top.
2. A similar tramp to the Waipakahi Valley and then over Middle Range on the Thunderbolt Track. Both these tramps are for experienced trampers.
3. From Waiouru over Defence Force land. Access is restricted; ask permission.
4. By walking upstream from the Taihape–Napier Road.
5. By helicopter from Taupo, Turangi or Taihape.
6. Helicopter access is not permitted in the wilderness section upstream from the Otamateanui confluence.

☐ Season and restrictions

Above the Mangaohane (Matawhero) Bridge, 1 October–30 April. Below the Mangaohane Bridge, the river is open for fishing all year. In the wilderness section upstream from the Otarere confluence, only one trout may be taken and it must be less than 55 cm in length.

Between the Otarere Stream confluence and the Mangaohane Bridge, four fish may be taken but all must be less than 55 cm. Artificial fly or spinner only is permitted above the Mangaohane Bridge.

The wilderness section and upper reaches north of the Taihape–Napier Road are a unique trophy fishery, hence the restrictions on the size and number of fish that can be taken. If any trout taken are tagged, return these tags to the Wellington Fish and Game Council with full details (see p 21).

In recent years the average length and weight of trout have fallen and double-figure fish (over 4.5 kg or 10 lb) are now rare. The cause of this decline is at present unknown. The upper Rangitikei contains larger and older fish than any other river in New Zealand; the only other similar fishery is the upper Ruakituri River. Overseas anglers and guides frequently visit the upper reaches by helicopter and raft in search of a trophy.

This valley is very exposed to the south and extremely cold in winter. The river winds through the heavily bushclad mountains of the Kaimanawa Forest Park. There are sheltered campsites in the valley, and Ecology Stream and the Mangamaire River confluences are popular. Fish numbers thin out somewhat around 2 km upstream from Ecology Stream.

This is a medium-sized river in the wilderness section and although there are some large deep pools, it can be forded in low-water conditions. Some crossings may be deep, however, and the rock and stone riverbed can be slippery. The water is very clear and seldom discolours with rain. Trout can be sighted, but are very wary as their vision is extremely good, especially in the deeper, slower-flowing pools. It is frequently difficult to reach fish from below and it is not unusual to find the majority lying in deep water two-thirds of the way down the pool but still out of casting distance from the tail. Occasionally, on a bright, calm, sunny day when the fishing pressure is minimal, trout feed along the edges of runs. Once disturbed, however, it may be one or two days before they resume feeding.

Fish can be taken on well sunk nymphs, lures, dry flies and spinners. A sinking line fished downstream with a long trace and two heavy nymphs may be needed to reach difficult fish. Most of the trout in these upper reaches are rainbows. There are a few very large browns, with the brown trout population increasing gradually over recent years. Be prepared to hike off downstream when you hook a good fish as they are robust fighters.

MOHAKA RIVER

☐ Location

The headwater tributaries, Oamaru, Kaipo and Taharua, join near Poronui to form the Mohaka River. The main river flows southeast through the Kaweka Forest Park for over 20 km before meeting the Ripia River near Pakaututu. The middle reaches then turn and flow northeast from Pakaututu to eventually reach the sea south of Wairoa, at the small settlement of Mohaka.

☐ Access to upper reaches

Access is not easy as there is a private fishing lodge on the Taharua River. There is a paper road (marked with poles) across Poronui Station, but it is a three-hour walk to the river.

1. For the tramping angler. A five to seven-hour tramp over Te Iringa Saddle from Clements Access Road off SH 5 to the Oamaru Hut, or a five to six-hour tramp over Waitawhero Saddle from the Boyd Hut and airstrip down the Oamaru Valley to the Oamaru Hut, then an hour's walk downstream to the Taharua confluence.
2. By fixed-wing aircraft from Taupo to the Oamaru, Otupae or 'Footy Field' airstrips. This is the easiest and most economical access.
3. By rafting the river with a commercial operator from Taupo.
4. Bt helicopter from Poronui.

☐ Access to middle reaches

1. From Pakaututu, north of Puketitiri. Just before the Pakaututu Bridge turn left onto Hot Springs–Makahu Road. This leads to the Blue Gums camping area at the road end, with access to the river. A tramping track follows further upstream.
2. From the Pakaututu Bridge over the Mohaka River.
3. SH 5 (the Napier–Taupo road) crosses the river 45 km north of Napier. McVickers Road follows upstream on the true left bank before crossing the river. Waitara Road follows downstream on the true right bank to Fisherman's Bend and the DoC camping ground at Glenfalls.
4. Pohokura Road, from Tutira on SH 2 north of Napier, leads eventually to the river opposite the Te Hoe River confluence.
5. Willow Flat Road leaves SH 2 near Kotemaori.

☐ **Access to lower reaches**
SH 2 crosses near the mouth at Raupunga.

☐ **Season and restrictions**
Above the Mangatainoka confluence, 1 October–30 April.

Below this confluence the river (excluding all tributaries) is open for fishing all year. The daily bag limit upstream from SH 5 bridge is one fish.

This large river, protected by a National Water Conservation Order (see Glossary, p 201) in its upper reaches, offers a wide variety of fishing and is the most popular fishing river in Hawke's Bay. Access, especially to the upper reaches, is difficult because of private ownership and rugged terrain. The river holds an excellent stock of mainly brown trout in the upper reaches above Pakaututu and mainly rainbow in the middle reaches below Pakaututu. These average 1.4 kg. However, there are trophy fish in this river and trout weighing 3 kg are not uncommon.

The upper wild and scenic reaches are best fished by adventurous tramper anglers. The riverbanks in the section below the Taharua confluence are overgrown by manuka scrub and beech forest interwined with bush lawyer (a thorny trailing plant) and are truly an angler's nightmare. There are some good campsites on the river, however. The river can be forded but rocks and stones are often slippery, and beware the gorgy sections. There is seldom any need to wade until a fish is spotted and then only to get into the correct position.

Trout are very receptive to a wide variety of dry flies, nymphs and spinners. As in many wilderness rivers, trout are not very selective, so the choice of fly pattern used is not so important as correct size, careful approach, accurate first cast, and drag-free float. The banks of the upper section are covered in bush and scrub and are stable, so the river seldom becomes discoloured after rain. If it does, it will become fishable again in a day or so.

NGARURORO RIVER

☐ Location

Drains the Kaimanawa and Kaweka forest parks and flows parallel to, but east of, the Rangitikei River in its upper reaches as far south as the Taihape–Napier Road at Kuripapango. Here the river turns east, leaves the Ruahine Range and flows over the Heretaunga Plains to share a mouth with the Tutaekuri River.

Only the upper reaches of this large river, upstream from the Taihape–Napier road, will be described.

☐ Access

1. By fixed-wing aircraft to the Boyd Hut at the headwaters of the river.
2. By walking upstream from Kuripapango where the Taihape–Napier road crosses the river. The first two fords can be deep and difficult unless the river is very low, so care should be taken.
3. If the river is unfordable, take the high-level tramping track to Cameron Hut (four to five hours, for tramper anglers only).

☐ Season and restrictions

Above the Taruarau confluence, 1 October–30 April. Below this confluence the river is open for fishing all year. Upstream of the Whanawhana cable, only one fish may be taken, and it must be between 35 and 55 cm in length.

The headwaters flow across exposed, open tussock country in the Kaimanawa Forest Park. There are usually a few fish above and below the Boyd airstrip, but fishing improves considerably 5 km downstream, near Panako (Gold) Creek. Here the river enters patchy manuka scrub with a few short, easily negotiated gorges. The pools are well developed and stable. The river is smaller than the upper Rangitikei and can be crossed at the tail of most pools. Clear water affords great visibility so fish are easy to spot and stalk – and just as easily spooked. There is a good stock of rainbows averaging 1.3 kg with an occasional fish up to 4 kg. Rafting is popular in this stretch of river down as far as Kuripapango.

The river immediately upstream from Kuripapango is very

gorgy with steep cliffs and difficult to negotiate except in low-water conditions. It is only suitable for fit, active anglers confident with river crossings. However, there is good fishing all the way to Cameron Hut and beyond. In this section it is a medium-sized river with some very deep pools.

An occasional fish can be sight-fished but likely-looking water should be fished blind with heavily weighted nymphs or an attractor pattern dry fly.

WAIRARAPA district

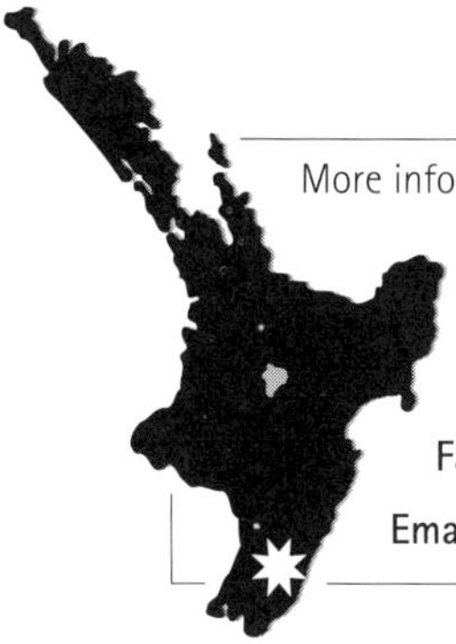

More information can be obtained from Tourism Wairarapa

Mail: PO Box 814, Masterton

Phone: (06) 378-7373

Fax: (06) 378-7042

Email: tourwai@xtra.co.nz

Wairarapa lies in the southeast of the North Island, about an hour and a half by car from Wellington. It is bordered by the rugged Rimutaka and Tararua ranges to the west and to the east by the Aorangi Range and rolling hill country leading to the Pacific Ocean. Summers are warm and dry.

There is a wide variety of exciting outdoor activities, interesting shops and museums in the small country towns, and excellent wineries in the Martinborough area. Golfers are well catered for, with good courses at Masterton, Carterton and Martinborough. The Wairarapa is also renowned for its gardens and nurseries, and these are well worth a visit.

Accommodation includes budget backpackers, camping grounds and cabins, homestays and farmstays, bed and breakfasts, motels with facilities, and hotels. There are also luxury lodges, country houses and rural retreats.

The Mt Bruce National Wildlife Centre, 25 minutes' drive north of Masterton, displays live takahe, kiwi, kokako and tuatara. The Wairarapa coast is wild and rugged, but there are great walks there and in the Tararua Forest Park.

There are sports stores in most small country towns where local angling information can be obtained. However, the tackle selection may be limited.

RIVERS

MANAWATU RIVER

☐ Location

This popular large river drains southern Hawke's Bay, the southern Ruahine Range and the northern Tararua Range. It follows a southerly course to Dannevirke, where it turns east and then enters the Manawatu Gorge 8 km east of Woodville. It emerges near Ashhurst and meanders across farmland, past Palmerston North to reach the sea at Foxton Beach.

☐ Access

Roads follow the river quite closely along most of its course. Suggested roads to take include Kopua Road, which leaves SH 2 just south of the Manawatu Bridge between Takapau and Norsewood; Garfield Road (19 km north of Dannevirke) to Makotuku, then Donghi or Rakaitai roads; and Oringi Road (10 km south of Dannevirke). Permission is required to cross private farmland.

☐ Season and restrictions

Upstream of its confluence with the Mangatewainui Stream near Ormondville, 1 October–30 April. Elsewhere, 1 October–30 September. Bag limit is one trout above the Mangatewainui Stream, and four trout below this confluence.

Above Dannevirke there is excellent fly water. The river lies east of SH 2 and the upper reaches cross the highway just north of Norsewood. Fish can be spotted and stalked with dry fly and nymph, and brown trout up to 2 kg are not uncommon. There are good pools and runs through willows and farmland, and the river can be easily waded and crossed because it is not too big. Eutrophication can cause problems in hot summer conditions. The banks are generally clear for casting.

The stretch of water between Oringi and Dannevirke contains a very high fish population. The river here has a shingle and mud bed with large, deep pools, long glides and wide shingle riffles. Trout are difficult to spot but wading is safe. Crossings are possible at the tail of pools, provided care is taken. There is good sedge fishing on warm summer evenings using a soft-hackle wet fly or a deer-hair sedge. Emerger patterns can prove deadly.

Downstream of Woodville the water is heavy and better suited to wet-fly fishing and spinning. The gorge does not hold many fish. At Ashhurst the river is heavily fished by all legal methods including dry and wet fly, nymph, spinner and live bait. More recently, anglers have adopted Taupo techniques, using two weighted nymphs or a high-density line and lure. Others have been successful with a nymph sunk with the aid of split shot and cast with a spinning rod. The mouth of Kahuterawa Stream and the water near Linton Camp both hold good fish in April and May when the spawning run begins.

The water quality deteriorates at Opiki and the lower 20 km are tidal.

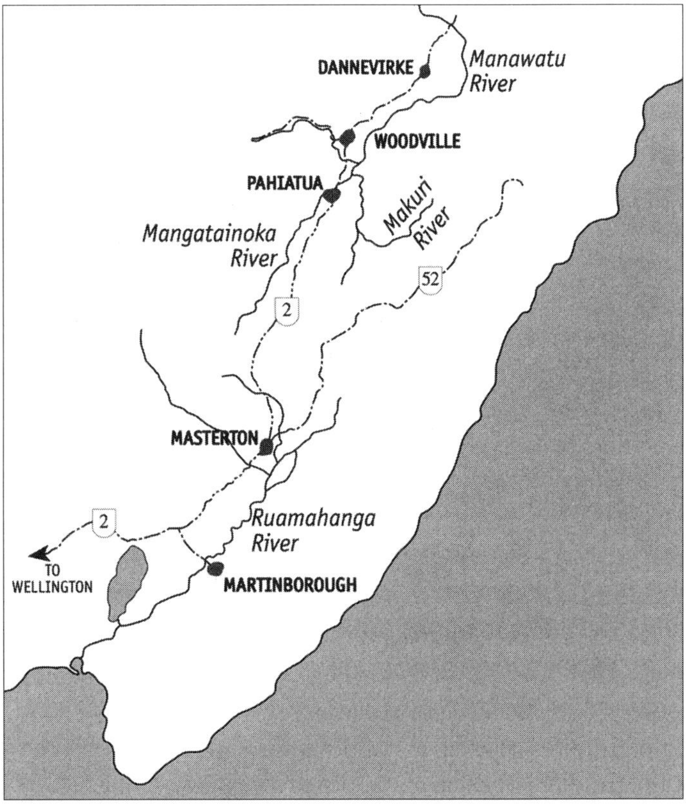

Wairarapa district

MANGATAINOKA RIVER

☐ Location

Flows parallel to, and between, SH 2 in the east and the Mangahao River in the west. Enters the Manawatu south of Woodville near Ngawapurua.

☐ Access

There is road access west of SH 2 at successive turn-offs to Mangamutu, at Konini, to Mangamaire and to Hukanui from Hamua. The Magatainoka Valley Road can be reached west of Eketahuna. SH 2 crosses the river at Mangatainoka, close to the brewery.

☐ Season and restrictions

Above the Makakahi confluence, 1 October–30 April. Elsewhere, 1 October–30 September. There is no bag limit.

This large river is highly rated and heavily fished. It has been protected by a water conservation order and fish stocks are good. The riverbed is shingle and the low, willow-lined banks generally permit unobstructed flycasting on one side. There are well defined pools and long glides. Crossings are generally not difficult, although the stony bed can be slippery. There is approximately 45 km of fishable water. The middle and lower reaches are the most productive and hold slightly larger fish than the upper reaches. Above Hukanui, the river is unstable and prone to changing course in floods. Following the onset of warm temperatures most of the trout drop back downstream.

There is often a good evening rise and fish can be spotted and stalked in the middle and upper reaches. There is excellent water adjacent to the brewery. Try size 12–14 Pheasant Tail, Halfback, Hare's Ear or Midge Pupa nymphs during the day, along with Coch-y-bondhu, Adams and Dad's Favourite dry flies. In the evening it is hard to go past Twilight Beauty in sizes 12–14 or a deer-hair sedge. Soft-hackle wet flies are very effective. Browns in the 0.75–2 kg range can be expected.

MAKURI RIVER

☐ Location

Drains the Waewaepa and Puketoi ranges, east of Pahiatua. The river flows in a southwesterly direction but just south of Makuri turns north to enter the Tiraumea River at Ngaturi.

☐ Access

East of Pahiatua on the Ngaturi–Makuri road. The season is 1 October–30 April. Above the Makuri township bridge, fly and spin fishing only are permitted.

☐ Season and restrictions

1 October–30 April. Bag limit is one trout.

This small tributary of the Tiraumea River is highly rated by fly anglers. Some years ago, Hardy's of London named one of their fly rods after this river, such was its reputation. The most popular stretch lies in the region of Makuri village, where the willow-lined stream wanders across farmland. Trout are easily spotted and just as easily frightened, so a careful approach and a fine tippet are essential for success. This is especially true after Christmas owing to the high numbers of anglers during the holiday season. Early morning is often the best time to fish. Fish fight well and have a tendency to tangle in the willow roots. A kilometre upstream from the Domain the river is more difficult to fish because of overhanging scrub. Downstream, in the region of the gorge, limestone sinkholes, large boulders and native bush provide considerable interest for the fit angler. Boots and shorts are recommended for this rough stretch of water, where there are some large browns. Try a well weighted stonefly nymph. Good fishing continues for 1 km below the gorge, then the river becomes sluggish and uninteresting. Although some anglers believe this river has deteriorated over the past 20 years, drift dives by Fish and Game Council officers have been reassuring and some excellent fish up to 3 kg have been seen. As a result of clear-felling in the headwaters, this river easily becomes silt-laden in a fresh. There is basic camping in the Makuri Domain.

RUAMAHANGA RIVER

☐ **Location**

Rises in the Tararua Range northwest of Masterton, flows in a southerly direction just east of Masterton and empties into Lake Onoke at Palliser Bay.

☐ **Access**

UPPER REACHES: The river flows parallel to, but east of, SH 2 from Mt Bruce to Masterton. The stretch in the bush-covered Tararua Range can only be reached by tramping across private farmland (permission required).

MIDDLE REACHES: From the Masterton–Gladstone road; from Papawai and Morrisons Bush, southeast of Greytown; from Martinborough.

LOWER REACHES: From the Martinborough–Lake Ferry road.

☐ **Season and restrictions**

1 October–30 September downstream from the Tararua Forest Park boundary. 1 October–30 April above this point. There is no bag limit.

This large river is popular because of the good catch rate, large area of fishable water and easy access. It has a wide shingle bed with long glides and riffles. Willows line the banks in some stretches, but wading is safe. Near Masterton there are cliffs lining the banks.

The middle reaches are the most heavily fished and brown trout weighing 0.5–3 kg can be taken on fly, spinner or live bait. This river is well stocked and in favourable conditions an excellent evening rise occurs. Recently rainbow trout up to 1.5 kg have been caught around Masterton and downstream to Gladstone. It is thought these may have escaped from Henley Lake in Masterton, which has been stocked for junior anglers.

Favoured locations include Wardells Bridge east of Masterton, the cliffs area just south of Masterton, Te Whiti Bridge and Ponatahi Bridge. In the headwaters above Mt Bruce there is always the chance of a trophy fish. From Mt Bruce downstream to Masterton the river is very unstable and subject to shingle extraction. Below Tuhitarata the river is deep, slow-flowing and sluggish, but local anglers get results by slow trolling. A few large sea-run browns (up to 6 kg) enter the river during February and March but these are hard to catch. Perch up to 1.5 kg are present in the river up as far as Masterton and will take any kind of trout lure. In a fresh the river rapidly becomes silt-laden and takes time to clear.

Try Caddis, Red-tipped Governor, Willow Grub and dark Hare and Copper or Hare's Ear nymphs, Dad's Favourite, Parachute Adams, Coch-y-bondhu and Twilight Beauty dry flies, or Hamill's Killer and small Yellow Rabbit lures. For the spin angler, Veltic, Meps and Cobra will take fish. The lower reaches are generally fished with spinning gear, while the upper reaches offer good fishing for the adventurous fly angler prepared to walk.

There are many other smaller streams and tributaries of the rivers described above that are also worth exploring. These include the upper reaches of the Waiohine and Waingawa, the Makakahi and the Kopuaranga rivers; also the Kourarau Dam. For additional information, check at the local sports stores or refer to John Kent, *North Island Trout Fishing Guide* (Reed, 2000).

For more information contact:

Nelson Visitor Information Centre
Mail: PO Box 194, Nelson
Phone: (03) 548-2304
Fax: (03) 546-7393
Email: vin@latitudenelson.co.nz

Blenheim Information Centre
Mail: PO Box 880, Blenheim
Phone: (03) 578-9904
Fax: (03) 578-6084
Email: blm-info@clear.net.nz

With high sunshine hours, warm, safe beaches and beautiful landscapes, the small city of Nelson (pop. 35,000) is a favourite destination for both local and overseas holidaymakers. A relaxed lifestyle has attracted potters, artists, woodturners and glassblowers, and their crafts are exhibited in a number of galleries. There is a wide range of restaurants and cafés. Nelson scallops are notable and the locally grown berryfruits should not be overlooked.

Major events in the area include the Nelson Jazz Festival (late December), the Gentle Annie Craft Fair (1 January), the Air New Zealand Mardi Gras (mid January), and Taste Nelson (last weekend in January).

Outdoor activities in this region include caving, sea kayaking, golfing, hiking, skydiving, horse trekking, sea fishing, diving, yachting and rock climbing. Tramping the Abel Tasman, Kahurangi and Nelson Lakes national parks is a preferred activity for the fit and active. Tours of historic homes and gardens, local vineyards and boutique breweries should be high on the list of priorities when you are not angling.

Accommodation of every description is available but advance booking is advisable during the summer season (December through March).

Tackle shops are located in the towns and professional guides are available for hire. As the demand may be high over the summer months we suggest booking well in advance.

The Marlborough region is famous for its vineyards and olive groves and a wine tour with lunch at a vineyard should not be missed. There is a wide variety of white and red wines; and the pinot noir and sauvignon blanc, which are regional specialties, have received worldwide acclaim. In summer, the sunshine hours are long and the evenings warm and pleasant.

Karamea, Mokihinui and tributaries

Both the Karamea and Mokihinui rivers lie in the West Coast Fish and Game Council region, but as access is generally easier from Nelson they are included in this section.

KARAMEA RIVER

☐ Location

The main river rises where the Allen Range saddles with the Little Wanganui and Wangapeka rivers. Initially the river flows north through heavily bushclad hills, but at the Leslie River confluence (Big Bend) it turns west, eventually reaching the Tasman Sea at Karamea township.

☐ Access

HEADWATERS: From the Wangapeka track, a two-day tramp to Luna Hut.

UPPER REACHES: By tramping downstream from Luna Hut.

FROM THE GRAHAM VALLEY NEAR NGATIMOTI: A two-day tramp over the Mt Arthur tableland and down the Leslie Valley.

FROM THE BATON VALLEY: A long day's tramp over the Baton Saddle to the Leslie Valley and Big Bend.

FROM THE COBB VALLEY: a two- to three-day tramp via Lake Peel and Balloon Hut on the Mt Arthur tableland to Big Bend.

MIDDLE REACHES: By tramping downstream from Big Bend to the Roaring Lion Hut (five hours), or upstream from Karamea and the Greys Hut (two to three days) Both these routes are difficult.

LOWER REACHES: 11 km of the lower reaches can be accessed through private farmland from Arapito or Umere roads. Upstream from here, a track follows the north bank of the river for an hour and a half; then trampers must walk the riverbed for another three hours to Grey's Hut (six bunks). This route is difficult unless the river is low. From here it is another day's tramp upriver to the mouth of the Ugly River.

Many overseas anglers fly in by helicopter from Nelson, Motueka or Karamea, while others tackle the river by raft (Grade 4).

☐ Season and restrictions

Open all year below a cableway at the mouth of the lower gorge. Above this point, 1 October–30 April. The bag limit above the cableway is two fish; below is four fish.

This is by far the largest river in the Kahurangi National Park. The main river and its many tributaries offer wonderful wilderness brown trout fishing, as good as it gets in New Zealand. From Luna Hut all the way to Karamea the main river provides an endless stock of self-sustaining fish averaging 2 kg.

The headwaters and upper reaches above the Leslie confluence flow rapidly over a rocky and stony bed. With 40 large fish per km above the Crow Hut, there is great nymph and dry-fly fishing for the agile boots-and-shorts angler. Some fish can be spotted, but the water is lightly tannin-stained and fish lying in the deeper slots can easily be missed. The river can be forded in places, provided care is taken, but by the time it reaches the Leslie River junction it is moderate in size and the pools are larger, deeper and slower. Here the population is about 50 large fish per km.

Near the Roaring Lion confluence lie the Earthquake Lakes, formed during the 1928 Murchison earthquake, and these are well stocked with both trout and eels. Spinning is especially effective as the lakes are too wide to cover with a fly rod. Watch for fish cruising the edges. Below the Roaring Lion, the country becomes very remote, the river gorgy and the angling pressure minimal. There is still great water, however.

The lower reaches at Karamea are large, slower-flowing and better suited to spinning, although trout can still be taken on a fly, especially during the evening rise. Drift dives at Arapito reveal good stocks (100 fish per km) of mainly medium-sized trout.

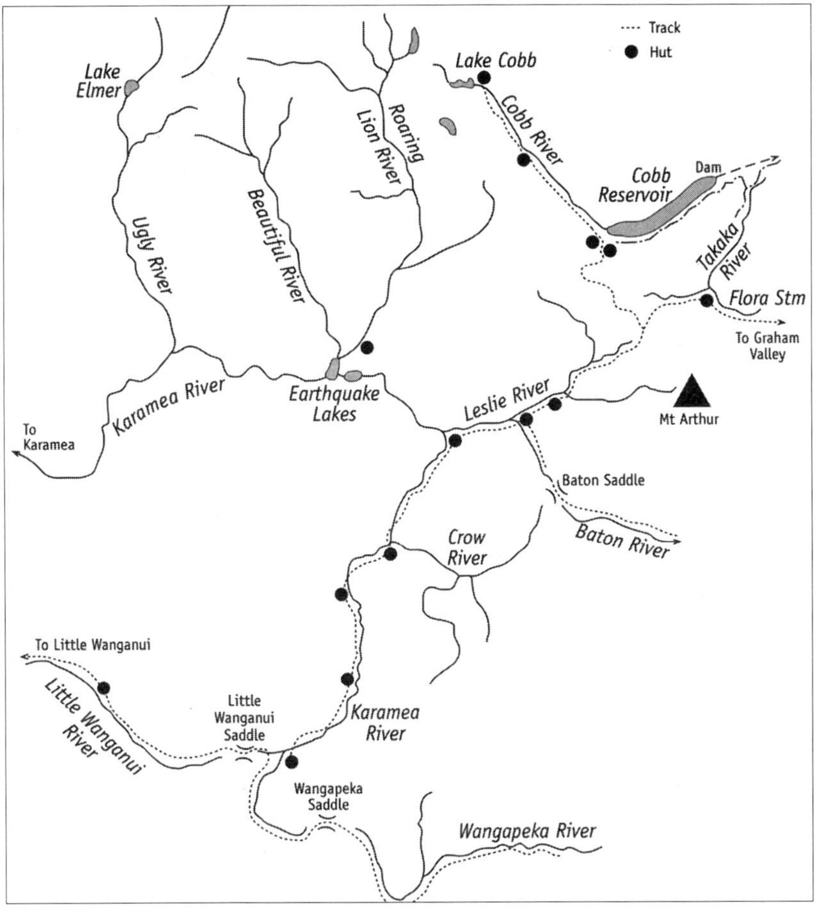

Karamea River system

KARAMEA TRIBUTARIES

All reasonable-sized tributaries contain trout but only the five most important ones will be described here. They all have the same season and regulations as for the upper Karamea: 1 October–30 April; bag limit two trout.

Crow River

☐ Access

See Karamea River, above. The Crow Hut at the Karamea/Crow confluence offers 'back-country accommodation' and a base for fishing this remote small to medium-sized clear-water tributary.

The river flows west and holds good numbers of fish that are easily spotted on a sunny day. Fish are generally not sophisticated feeders and will accept a large variety of dries and nymphs if they are carefully presented. Wear overtrousers and long sleeves for protection from sandflies.

There are two days' worth of fishing upstream from the Karamea confluence but the going is difficult in places. The riverbed boulders are large and slippery, there are gorgy sections and the bush needs to be entered in order to negotiate some stretches of river. Some pools are very deep.

Leslie River

☐ Access

See Karamea River, above. This is the most accessible tributary, and the Karamea Bend Hut is the best base. The Leslie Hut has recently burned down.

The river is small and easily waded and crossed but there are some deep holes. As with all the tributaries, the Leslie is bush-lined, with clear water and a rock and stone riverbed. There is a good day's fishing upstream from the mouth.

Roaring Lion River

☐ Access

See Karamea River, above. A hard five to six-hour tramp downriver from Big Bend to Roaring Lion Hut. From the Cobb Valley either via Kimbell Spur or from Chaffey Hut via Chaffey Stream and Breakfast Creek (seven to nine hours). From the Ugly or Aorere headwaters via Aorere Saddle. These routes are for experienced trampers only. Otherwise, by helicopter to Roaring Lion Hut.

This is a marvellous medium-sized remote river offering similar conditions to the Crow and Leslie rivers, but the river is larger and fords are tricky in the lower reaches – some are more than waist-deep. The river flows south through heavily bushclad mountains. There are trophy fish in this river, although fishing pressure from anglers coming by helicopter has made the fish more wary. Good fishing is available up as far as Breakfast Creek, a long day's tramp from the Roaring Lion Hut near the mouth.

Beautiful River

□ Access

See Karamea River, above. This small tributary can easily be reached across from the Roaring Lion Hut, provided the Roaring Lion is fordable. Only the lower 1–2 km are worth fishing, with a few good pools before the river rises steeply and the going gets rough.

Ugly River

□ Access

See Karamea River, above. This is the most remote tributary and only experienced trampers should attempt to reach it – upriver from Karamea, downriver from the Roaring Lion Hut, or via the saddle between the Roaring Lion and Ugly headwaters. It is slightly smaller than the Roaring Lion and flows south from its source at Lake Elmer. The east branch joins a few kilometres below the lake.

There are good stocks of brown trout that can be sight-fished, with the best water lying between McNabb and Domett creeks. The river floods easily but also clears rapidly. Holds the odd trophy fish in the headwaters.

The Cawthron Institute conducted research on trout behaviour in 1999 on this river. They found that spooked trout took at least 24 hours to reappear from their hiding places and fish that had been caught and released remained hidden for up to three days. Trout were also wary of a fly they had previously taken and were resistant to accepting that pattern a second time.

MOKIHINUI RIVER

☐ Location

This river drains a very large catchment of rugged bush country, including the Radiant, Allen, Matiri and Lyell ranges. The north and south branches respectively flow north and south to The Forks. The main river then flows west to enter the sea at Mokihinui, some 40 km north of Westport.

☐ Access

LOWER REACHES: Along SH 67 and the Mokihinui–Seddonville road there is access to 11 km of the lower reaches. Beyond Seddonville, a 4WD is advisable.

MIDDLE REACHES: Tramp upstream on a track at the end of the Mokihinui–Seddonville road and follow the south bank of the river. This track has been washed out and some areas have become very treacherous, especially crossing slips. It is due for repair.

UPPER REACHES: By tramping over Kiwi Saddle into the Johnson tributary from the Wangapeka Track.

The Forks Hut (six bunks) is seven to eight hours' tramp from the road end, and many anglers and hunters fly in by helicopter from Karamea or Motueka. Sinclair Hut (four bunks) on the north branch is only 30 minutes' walk across the river flats from Forks Hut. There is also a hut on the Johnson River. On the south branch, Goat Creek Hut, opposite Hennessy Creek, is three hours' tramp from Forks, and sleeps four. An update on the condition of these huts should be obtained from DoC before embarking on a trip to this remote watershed. If in any doubt, carry a tent.

☐ Season and restrictions

Open all year below a cableway near Welcome Creek. Above the cableway, 1 October–30 April. The bag limit for the main river and tributaries above the cableway is two trout; below the cableway is four trout.

This is a superb remote brown trout fishery, somewhat smaller than its northern neighbour, the Karamea. In the upper reaches and tributaries there are extensive stretches of clear, rocky and stony mountain water with fish averaging 2 kg (30 large trout per km in the north and south branches). It is pointless just fishing the water in these upper reaches, as most feeding fish can be easily seen. This scenic river and its tributaries flow down valleys of beech bush and tussock flats. All major tributaries hold fish, with the Johnson, Allen, Hemphill, Larrikin and Hennessy creeks especially recommended. The river can flood in dramatic fashion after heavy rain so that, at times, the flats at the Forks resemble a lake, but generally the upper reaches clear rapidly afterwards.

The middle reaches are more difficult to access and the river is much larger. However, there are still plenty of trout to entice the fit and active angler. The lower reaches offer sea-run fish, especially during the whitebait season in spring. These can be caught on spinners or a smelt fly.

RIWAKA RIVER

☐ Location

The north branch emerges from a deep, dark-blue spring on the Takaka Hill south of Riwaka township. After joining up with its south branch, the main stream flows east through farmland and enters Tasman Bay just north of Motueka.

☐ Access

The scenic Riwaka River Valley road leaves SH 60 at the foot of Takaka Hill and follows up the true left bank of the main stream and up both branches for a short distance. It is a short scramble to the stream.

☐ Season and restrictions

1 October–30 April. Artificial bait and fly only. Bag limit is two trout, and only one longer than 50 cm can be taken.

This small, clear, shingly stream is overhung by willows and other vegetation in some stretches but is generally a delight to fish. Drift dives near the Moss Bush picnic area have found good numbers of takeable brown trout of 0.5–1.2 kg. Wading is safe, although the algae-covered stones are slippery. Fish are not easy to spot on the brownish riverbed so many runs should be fished blind. In late summer, willow grub and lace moth imitations are a good choice to use, but any small nymph or dry fly should entice a take.

MOTUEKA RIVER AND TRIBUTARIES

Motueka River

☐ **Location**

Drains the Richmond Range to the east, the Hope and Lookout ranges to the south, and the Mt Arthur Range to the west. Flows generally north for 60 km, through Motupiko and Ngatimoti to Tasman Bay, just north of Motueka.

☐ **Access**

The river is well served with roads, especially on the true right bank, from the gorge and Golden Downs Forest to its mouth. SH 61 follows the river upstream on the east bank from Motueka to SH 6 at Kohatu. On the west (true left) bank, West Bank Road follows upstream from SH 60 close to the Baton River, with access at various points. Near Tapawera, the lower Wangapeka Road follows downstream to the Wangapeka River confluence. Valley Road follows the river upstream from Kohatu through Golden Downs Forest to the gorge above Janson Bridge. Numerous angler accesses are clearly marked on all these roads. Elsewhere, be sure to ask permission before crossing private land.

☐ **Season and restrictions**

Above the Ngatimoti bridge, 1 October–30 April. Below this bridge, the river is open all year. The bag limit above the Wangapeka confluence is two trout, only one of which may exceed 50 cm. Below this confluence the limit is also two trout.

Despite being heavily fished, this moderate-sized river, an hour's drive from Nelson, holds an abundance of brown trout averaging around 1 kg, with fish up to 3 kg occasionally taken. Stocks vary from season to season, but as many as 275 trout per kilometre of river have been counted at Woodstock. Both resident and sea-run trout are present, with the larger fish favouring the river upstream from the Wangapeka confluence. The lower and middle reaches offer long glides and riffles flowing over a gravel bed. There are some deep holes and rocky shelves, especially under the willows, which provide excellent stable trout habitat. Many of the larger fish wait until evening before emerging from these sheltered depths to feed. The river can flood but the water is normally clear enough to enable some daytime sight fishing. However, many riffles and runs should be fished blind, such is the extent of the fish population. Wading is safe and crossings can be made in selected spots along the middle and upper reaches.

On bright, sunny days, fishing can be challenging, although small well presented dry flies and nymphs imitating mayflies and caddis, fished on a long fine tippet, should prove successful. A willow grub imitation can be useful later in summer. In the evening, caddis (sedge) fishing can be very exciting with a soft-hackle wet-fly fished across and down on a floating line. Use a stronger tippet at night, as some of the takes can be fierce. This type of fishing is great for beginners, as results are easier to obtain than during the day.

The spin angler should try a small Veltic, a gold or silver Toby or a Mepps, and fish the deeper runs beneath the willows. Spinning is best after a fresh and becomes more difficult in low-water summer conditions.

Motupiko River

☐ Location

Rises near Top House, drains the area north of Lake Rotoiti and flows north to join the Motueka River at Kohatu.

☐ Access

SH 6 follows this river upstream from Kohatu, but a short walk across private farmland is sometimes necessary. Public access is available at Quinneys Bush Reserve, Long Gully (4 km from Kohatu off SH 6), Korere bridge, and the Rainy River road bridge.

☐ Season and restrictions

1 October–30 April. Artificial bait and fly only. Bag limit is two trout and only one fish longer than 50 cm may be taken.

This is a spawning tributary of the Motueka River and is similar in character to the parent river but much smaller. Best fished early in the season before fish drop back as water flows diminish in long hot summers. During the 1998 drought the river virtually ran dry. The first 5 km above the confluence holds the most fish, and these can be sighted and stalked. As the season progresses the fish become very spooky and, when frightened, will bolt for the deeper runs against the cliffs. Stocks are not high and catch and release is recommended.

Wangapeka River

☐ Location

Drains the area south of the Arthur Range, including parts of the Marino Range and Lookout Range in the Kahurangi National Park. Flows generally northeast and enters the Motueka River 7 km downstream from Tapawera.

☐ Access

The lower reaches can be reached by taking the Lower Wangapeka Road from Tapawera, which follows down the true left bank of the Motueka River to the confluence. From here, the road turns south and follows up the Wangapeka River, eventually crossing it at Cylinder Bridge. There are many accesses along this road. The middle and upper reaches are accessed from the Upper Wangapeka Road, where again many angler accesses are marked. It is possible to drive to Rolling River by 4WD vehicle, but this is over private farmland and permission must be obtained. The Kahurangi National Park begins above Rolling River and tramper anglers can continue exploring upstream along the Wangapeka Track.

☐ Season and restrictions

1 October–30 April. Bag limit is two fish, only one of which may exceed 50 cm.

This is a popular small to medium-sized rocky and stony river with its headwaters in stable, bush-covered hills. The trout numbers are not high in the headwaters but the quality of the angling experience more than compensates for this. Fish up to 2.5 kg have been taken and as the water is very clear, sight fishing is the preferred method.

The middle and lower reaches, holding a greater fish population, flow through farmland and bracken-covered hills. Fish can be spotted and stalked in bright, sunny conditions. The banks are stable and there is a succession of pools and runs but the river discolours readily in a fresh. It is best fished early in the season before resident fish become too wary or recovered spawners drop back downstream to the parent river.

PELORUS RIVER

☐ Location

Drains the Richmond and Bryant ranges. Flows north from the Mt Richmond State Forest Park, then east past Canvastown, to enter Pelorus Sound near Havelock.

☐ Access

UPPER REACHES: Take Mangatapu Road off SH 6 near Pelorus Bridge. This road goes upstream for 14 km to a carpark at Larges Clearing, with a number of access points along the way. From the carpark, a DoC track leads into the Mt Richmond Forest Park. Captain's Hut is four hours' tramp from the carpark and Midday Hut a six-hour tramp. There is little fishing beyond this point.

MIDDLE AND LOWER REACHES: SH 6 follows the river between Havelock and Pelorus Bridge, with numerous marked angler accesses. At Daltons Bridge, Kaiuma Road leads downstream on the north bank. Always get permission before crossing farmland.

☐ Season and restrictions

Above the Rai confluence, 1 October–30 April. Only two fish may be taken, with one only exceeding 50 cm. Below the Rai confluence, there is an open season and a bag limit of two fish.

The headwaters of the Pelorus River in the Mt Richmond Park hold only a few good-sized browns that are easy to spot in this small rocky and stony wilderness river.

Fish numbers are much greater below the Rai confluence, where the river swells, changes character and becomes quite large. There are long glides, deep runs beneath willows, and shallow, shingly riffles. Good stocks of trout are present – about 70 percent are browns and the rest rainbows. Fish are typically 0.75–1.5 kg, although occasionally they are over 3 kg. The river is safe to wade, even at night. An active evening rise is common in summer. During the day, small caddis and mayfly nymphs and dries will take fish. At night, try a soft-hackle wet fly or a deer-hair sedge fished across and downstream.

The lower tidal reaches below Canvastown surprisingly hold some large fish, but these are best tempted with a spinner. Many small rainbows are also present in this stretch of water.

RAI RIVER

☐ Location

The Rai River and its three feeder streams drain the hills west of the Marlborough Sounds and enter the Pelorus River at Pelorus Bridge.

☐ Access

SH 75 runs parallel to the river in the Rai Valley for 10 km above the falls and, along with side roads, offers easy access to the river. There are angler accesses at Rai Falls, Bulford Bridge, Raidale Farm Road, Ford Stream Bridge, Brown Stream Reserve, Opouri Valley Bridge, Tunakino Valley Bridge and Opouri Valley Road.

☐ Season and restrictions

1 October–30 April. The bag limit is two trout, and in the feeder rivers Ronga, Opouri and Tunakino, the bag limit is also two trout but only one of these may exceed 50 cm.

This medium-sized tributary of the Pelorus holds good stocks of rainbow and brown trout (200 fish per km of river above the falls). The stream flows across farmland and, in bright conditions, fish can be sighted and stalked. It is a challenging stream to fish because of its long, clear, slow-flowing glides and trees and scrub on the bank. Trout spook easily and scatter in all directions after a clumsy cast. Wading is generally unnecessary although the river can be readily forded in places. The riverbed is gravel and mud. It discolours readily after rain and the water becomes tea-coloured from the bush lining the feeder streams.

The Ronga and Opouri rivers also offer interesting fly fishing, especially early in the season, although willows are a problem on some stretches. All three tributaries form the main river at Carluke. Permission is required to cross private land. In long, hot summers, low water flows and dairy effluent can result in eutrophication. Fish tend to drop back to the main river in these conditions.

WAIRAU RIVER

☐ Location

From its source in the Raglan, Spenser and St Arnaud ranges, the large Wairau River flows northeast for 150 km down the Wairau Valley before discharging into Cloudy Bay near Blenheim.

☐ Access

HEADWATERS: From the south on the Hanmer Springs hydro road. From the north on the Rainbow Station road which links with the hydro road. Permission and a key must be obtained from Rainbow Station (phone (03) 5211-838) if you intend fishing beyond Six Mile Creek, as there is a locked gate.

The Rainbow Skifield road, off the Rainbow Station road, also offers access as far as Six Mile Creek. This road is open to the public only from December to February. A 4WD vehicle is an advantage on this road as it can be rough in parts after winter snows and there are fords.

UPPER AND MIDDLE REACHES: There are numerous marked angler accesses off SH 63, and off North Bank Road along the true left bank from the Renwick Bridge on SH 6. This section of river is generally easy to access.

LOWER REACHES: Roads run down both banks of the river between the SH 1 bridge and the Renwick bridge on SH 6. Many marked angler accesses make reaching the river relatively simple, especially from the ends of short side roads. Downstream from the SH 1 bridge the river splits into the diversion and the main channel. Both are easy to access from roads running down their north banks from SH 1.

☐ Season and restrictions

Above Wash Bridge on SH 63, 1 October–30 April. Below this bridge and including the diversion, the river is open to angling all year. Above Wash Bridge the limit is two trout, only one of which may exceed 50 cm. Artificial bait and fly only. Below the bridge, the bag limit is two sports fish (see Glossary, p 202). It is illegal to fish for salmon above Wash Bridge.

The Wairau River offers a variety of angling. In the headwaters, the river is a boisterous, clear, rocky and stony river suitable for sight fly fishing in summer. There is excellent water for 15 km above the locked gate at Six Mile Creek. Trout cannot always be spotted so do not walk past likely looking water without throwing the odd cast. There are some deep slots where fish can hide. Stocks are not high but brown trout over 4.5 kg are not uncommon.

In the upper reaches downstream from Six Mile Creek there is some delightful water almost down as far as Wash Bridge. The river is quite large and should be crossed with care. In high summer, fly fishing to large sighted browns can be very exciting in some of the bouldery runs but fishing pressure has increased over the past few years and trout become more wary as the season progresses. There are plenty of sheltered campsites, but take sandfly repellent. Native beech forest and mountains create a splendid scenic backdrop to this upper section of the valley.

The middle reaches downstream from Wash Bridge are braided and rather unstable. The riverbed is very wide, shingly and spread out, but there is some good holding water, generally where the river runs against the bank or under willows. As the braids change from year to year, some early-season exploration is required to find this likely-looking water. Once the river clears from snowmelt, the water quality and clarity are excellent. Although most fish are caught on spinners in this section, there is some worthwhile fly fishing.

In the lower reaches below Renwick, the braids coalesce into a single channel but the water is deep and heavy. Spinning accounts for most fish, although lure fishing at night can be productive, both in the river itself and in the diversion. Early in the season a whitebait lure fished across and down on a sinking line can be effective.

This large river holds both resident and sea-run browns, with a small run of quinnat (chinook) salmon appearing in February and March. Some large browns are landed in the lower reaches and salmon up to 8 kg have been caught.

SPRING CREEK

Location

Rises from springs northwest of Blenheim near Rapaura, flows northeast and enters the Wairau just north of SH 1 near the township of Spring Creek.

Access

This is difficult as the creek flows through private residential property and farmland. However, east of SH 1, Stop Bank Road leads to a reserve and you can walk to the mouth. SH 1 crosses upstream from the mouth and access is also available from O'Dwyers and Rapaura roads west of Spring Creek township. Be sure to ask permission from landowners before fishing.

Season and restrictions

1 October–30 April. Artificial bait and fly only; bag limit is two fish with only one exceeding 50 cm in length.

This deep, clear, weedy spring creek is a favourite with some anglers. Good-sized brown trout offer a real challenge. Although there are 25 large browns per kilometre of river, they are hard to catch, often hiding beneath banks of weed and only emerging in late evening to feed. Weed and snags also tip the odds in favour of the fish, so a landing net is very useful. The creek has grassy, willow-lined banks and generally remains clear after rain.

During the day cast small weighted nymphs or small mayfly and caddis dry flies on a long fine tippet to sighted fish. A black lure swung deep through some of the holes in late evening can be effective, provided you explore the terrain before nightfall. Trout over 4 kg have been landed.

For more information contact:

Nelson Visitor Information Centre

Mail: PO Box 194, Nelson

Phone: (03) 548-2304

Fax: (03) 546-7393

Email: vin@latitudenelson.co.nz

or the local information centre in Murchison

Murchison is a small country town serving a farming community. It is two hours south of Nelson by car. Scenic attractions include Lakes Rotoroa and Rotoiti, the Maruia Falls and the pleasant countryside. The landscape was much altered by the Murchison Earthquake of 1929. There is an active golf club and a gallery offering handcraft, pottery, jade and paintings. Additional recreational activities include whitewater rafting, kayaking, mountain biking, caving, tramping, bushwalking, gold panning, jetboating and hunting. Accommodation is adequate in the midtown hotels, motels and camping ground, and two luxury lodges are located just out of town. Dining out opportunities are limited.

Major events in the township include a Tree Hugging Festival in February and the Buller White Water Festival in March. There are no tackle shops or sports stores but a local professional fly fishing guide has flies for purchase. Additional equipment can be bought in Nelson.

Nelson Lakes National Park consists of 100,000 ha of rugged mountains and unspoilt native bush. It contains two major lakes and a number of exciting rivers. Sufficient snow falls in winter to provide skiing on Mt Robert, and summer temperatures warm the lakes for swimming and water sports.

Visitors should first visit the park headquarters at St Arnaud for maps, hut permits and general information. There are motel and camping facilities at both lakes and a trout-fishing lodge at Lake Rotoroa. Insect repellent for sandflies is strongly advised.

Lakes National Park

TRAVERS RIVER

☐ Location and access

Drains the St Arnaud and Travers ranges of Nelson Lakes National Park, and flows in a northerly direction down a very scenic valley to the southern end of Lake Rotoiti. There are well marked tramping tracks around the lake but the journey may take three to four hours. This time can be considerably shortened by hiring a water taxi to the Lake Head or Coldwater huts at the head of the lake.

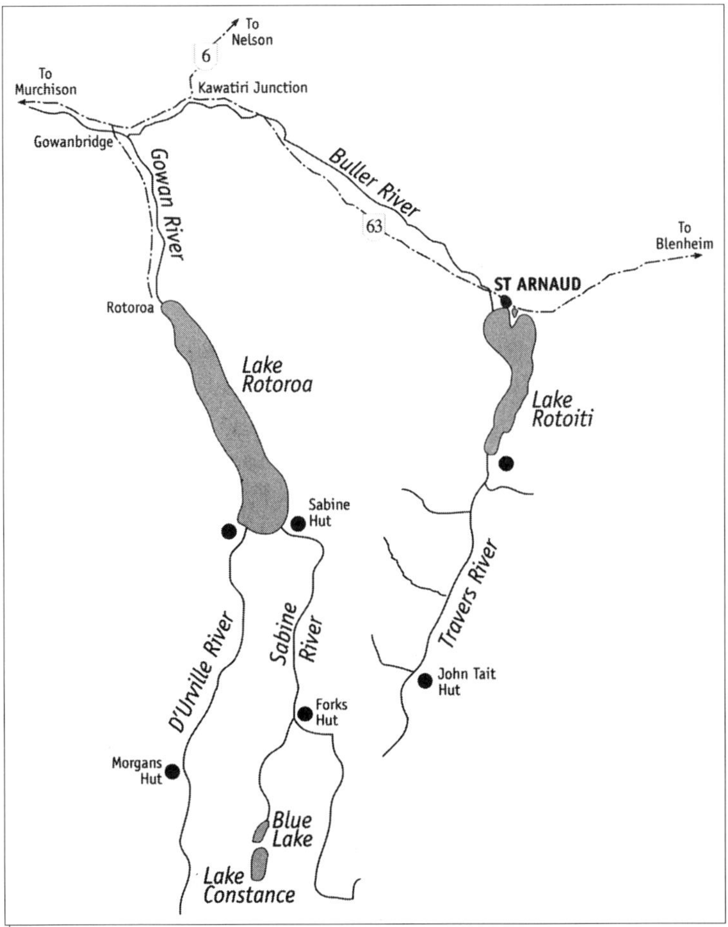

☐ **Season and restrictions**

1 October–30 April. Artificial bait or fly only; bag limit is two trout, with only one exceeding 50 cm in length.

This valley is worth visiting for the scenery alone, as the river winds across wide tussock flats edged with beech bush and overlooked by towering mountains. The river has a reasonably stable shingle bed and holds browns averaging 1.2 kg. These can be spotted and stalked in very clear, blue water for 10 km up the valley as far as the John Tait Hut. They become more and more spooky and selective as the season progresses, and require accurate casting, careful stalking and a drag-free presentation.

Try Coch-y-bondhu, Royal Wulff, Humpy, Irresistible and Black Gnat dry flies, and Hare and Copper, Halfback and Stonefly nymphs. If the trout seem spooky and no one is fishing ahead of you, reduce the fly size or increase the length of your tippet. Although this river is restocked from the lake, catch and release is recommended. On a calm, warm, sunny summer's day when the trout are feeding, the Travers is a dream river. You won't be alone, as the valley is popular with trampers.

SABINE RIVER

☐ **Location**

Drains the Spenser Mountains, Lake Constance (via an underground stream) and Blue Lake. Flows northwest and enters Lake Rotoroa east of the D'Urville mouth.

☐ **Access**

By water taxi to the head of the lake, or a six-hour tramp round the lakeshore. A marked track follows upriver on the true left bank; it is four to five hours' tramping to the Sabine Forks Hut. Permission to use these Parks Board huts should be obtained from the ranger station at St Arnaud.

☐ **Season and restrictions**

1 October–30 April. Artificial bait and fly only; bag limit two fish and only one of these may exceed 50 cm in length.

This clear, stony, wilderness river holds brown and rainbow trout with an occasional fish up to 3 kg. There are fish right up to the Sabine Forks but few upstream from that point. Sight-fishing is possible on some sections but do not neglect fishing the faster, deeper runs where fish are difficult to spot. The lower, unfishable gorge usually holds some large fish to tantalise anglers. The river clears rapidly after rain.

Lake Constance and the Blue Lake are worth visiting for the scenery but contain no fish.

D'URVILLE RIVER

☐ Location and access

The D'Urville mouth can be reached by following round the lakeshore from the wharf at Sabine Hut. A marked trampers' track follows upriver. Restrictions are as for the Sabine River.

The D'Urville flows down an attractive bush-covered valley parallel to, but west of, the Sabine. By contrast, this river holds mainly brown trout, which can normally be spotted under bright conditions. During some summers the river flow becomes so diminished that some fish return to the lake. It is best fished early in the season. There is 12 km of fishable water, up to well above Morgan's Hut. As with the Sabine, careful stalking, drag-free presentation and size of the fly are more important than the pattern. These fish are normally not selective unless recently fished over.

BULLER RIVER (UPPER REACHES)

☐ Location

Drains Lake Rotoiti, flows west to Kawatiri Junction then turns and flows south to Murchison. Below the inaccessible Upper Buller Gorge at Lyell, the river enters the West Coast Fish and Game Council region.

☐ Access

SH 6 follows the river upstream from Murchison to Kawatiri Junction. SH 63 follows on up the river to Lake Rotoiti.

There are 28 marked angler accesses on both these roads,

including: the outlet at the Nelson Lakes National Park camping ground, the end of Teetotal Road on the true right bank, Upper Buller Bridge, Speargrass Creek, Homestead Creek, Howard River confluence, Baigents Road, Windy Point, Kawatiri Junction, Washout Creek, Gowan Bridge, Granity Creek, Raits Bridge, Owen Domain, Matiri Valley Road, Murchison Motor Camp, Matakitaki Bridge and Hinehaka Road. A walk is often required to reach the river. Between the Mangles and Owen rivers access is through private farms but permission is seldom refused. There are camping grounds and campsites at Lake Rotoiti, Kawatiri Junction, Gowan Valley, Owen Domain and at Murchison.

☐ **Season and restrictions**

Above Gowan Bridge, 1 October–30 April; the bag limit is two fish. Below Gowan Bridge the river is open all year and the bag limit is also two fish.

Above the Gowan confluence, the Buller is a moderate-sized river and can be crossed in places, with care. Further down it swells into a large river and unless water flows are very low, crossings can be hazardous. Although the algae-covered stones provide good trout habitat, they can be very slippery when wading. It is wise to carry a wading staff. The Buller is a highly regarded self-sustaining brown trout fishery holding good stocks of fish averaging 1.5 kg (33 large and 172 medium-sized fish per km). As the Buller drains Lake Rotoiti, it remains clear and fishable above the Howard confluence even after persistent rain.

The outlet offers good night-time sedge fishing. Downstream to Kawatiri Junction there is excellent water, with some sight fishing possible along the edges of runs. However, the more boisterous water should also be covered as many fish shelter behind rocks and are very difficult to spot. The Buller is not an easy river to fish and requires a degree of fitness to manage the fast runs and turbulent pocket water. Long casting and drag-free drifts increase the chances of success. Well weighted beadhead or stonefly-type nymphs and buoyant, highly visible deer-hair dry flies are a good choice for this water. The banks are grassy with the occasional clump of beech trees and patches of manuka scrub.

Below the Gowan confluence, where the river is large, there is still plenty of scope for fly fishing as most trout feed in less than a metre of water and along the edges of currents and runs. It is worth having a reel holding 100 m of backing as there are some big fish in this river and once they lie side-on against the current it can be very difficult to follow them downstream.

Around Murchison the river is very wide, deep and slow-flowing. During the day spinning is the best method but on warm summer evenings trout move out of the deep water to feed on caddis. A soft-hackle wet fly or a deer-hair sedge can be most effective. Listen for the splashy rise forms. Below Murchison there is very heavy water but trout are taken on flies as well as spinners. Winter fishing by hardy anglers using a sinking line and a Woolly Bugger yields some fish.

River Tributaries

Unless stated otherwise, the season is 1 October–30 April and the bag limit is two fish, only one of which may exceed 50 cm in length.

OWEN RIVER

☐ Location

Flows generally south from the Lookout Range and Mt Owen to join the Buller at Owen River Junction, near the Owen River Hotel on SH 6.

☐ Access

A gravel road follows up the Owen Valley from the bridge on SH 6. The Nelson/Marlborough Fish and Game Council has clearly marked angler accesses along this road. Beyond Brewery Creek, permission to fish further upstream must be obtained from the first farm across the creek. In some parts, blackberry, scrub, bracken and willows impede access to the river.

☐ Season and restrictions

1 October–30 April. The bag limit is two fish and only one of these may exceed 50 cm.

The Owen is a small, gentle, delightful stream to fish but excessive angling pressure in recent years has made the trout very wary. Although the water is lightly tannin-stained and overhung by native bush in some sections, fish can be spotted and stalked. An accurate, gentle presentation with the first cast is essential. The river is stable, with well developed pools and runs. Wading and crossing present no problems, although the stony riverbed can be slippery. The gorge is normally easy to negotiate and holds a good stock of brown trout averaging 1.5 kg, with fish up to 2.5 kg not uncommon. Because of the intense angling pressure, it is best early in the season. By mid summer, when the trout have been repeatedly fished over, they seek shelter in a hide during the day and often only emerge at night to feed.

MANGLES RIVER

☐ Location

Rises in the bushclad Braeburn Range. The Tiraumea, Tutaki and Te Wiriki tributaries join at Tutaki to form the Mangles, while the Blackwater joins further downstream. This small to medium-sized river then flows west through a gorge and enters the Buller River at Longford, a few kilometres north of Murchison.

☐ Access

The Tutaki Valley road leaves SH 6, 5 km north of Murchison, at Longford and follows the river upstream to Tutaki. Gravel roads then follow up both branches. There are many well marked 'Angler Access' signs, but permission is required to use other routes through private farmland. The river flows deep in an overgrown gorge for 10 km, but above the gorge access is much easier across farmland.

☐ Season and restrictions

1 October–30 April. The bag limit is two fish.

This popular small to medium-sized river holds a good stock of brown trout (130 fish per km in the gorge) averaging 1 kg with the occasional fish of 2.5 kg. The gorge is fishable only in low-water conditions and you need to be fit to tackle this section. Boots and shorts are advisable as the pools can be very deep and the rocks large and slippery. Native bush, scrub and blackberry

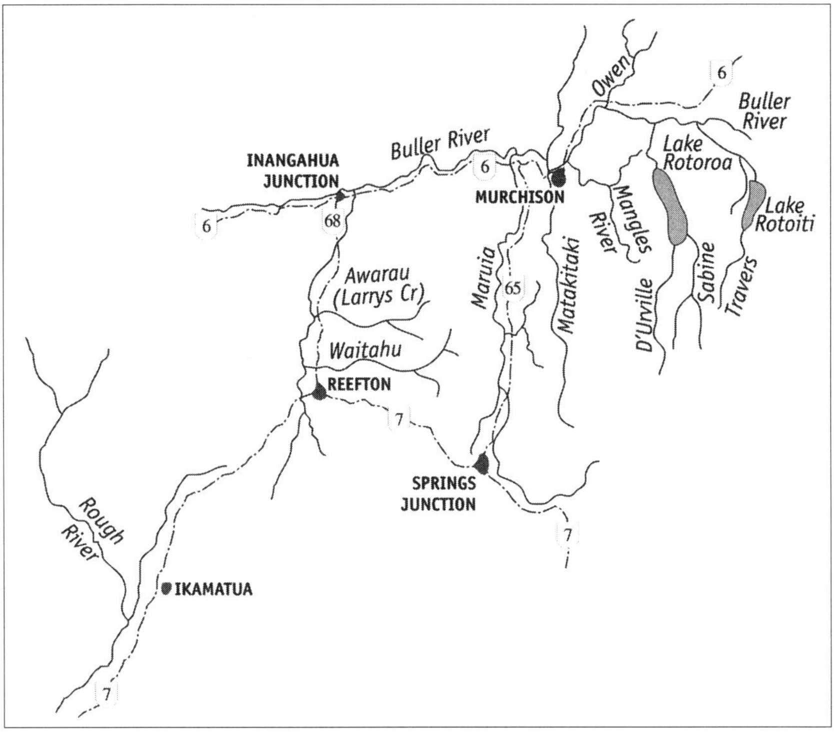

Murchison district

make the going tough in places. Trout are very difficult to spot in the gorge as the water is greenish-brown and turbulent in some stretches.

Above the gorge, the river is much more placid and easier to fish, but recent increased angler pressure has made the trout extremely wary, especially as the season progresses. There are stable pools and riffles and trout can be sight fished on a sunny day. The stream has a stable gravel bed that is ideal habitat for mayfly and caddis. There are patches of beech and scrub but the banks are mainly grassy, enabling unimpeded casting. The stream is easy to wade and cross here, although the stones are slippery.

Fish respond to small caddis and mayfly dry flies and nymphs, and the first cast must be accurate and delicate, as fish spook easily. It pays to carry a landing net. There can be a good evening rise in summer, and good-sized trout actively feeding on emergers.

Two tributaries, the Tutaki and Te Wiriki (Braeburn) rivers, also hold fish and are well worth a look, especially early in the season.

MATAKITAKI RIVER

☐ Location

Drains the Spenser Mountains and generally flows northwest to its confluence with the Buller River just south of Murchison.

☐ Access

UPPER REACHES: From the Mangles–Tutaki Valley road through Tutaki to the road end at Matakitaki Station. A tramping track follows up the true right bank to Downie Hut.

MIDDLE REACHES: From Murchison and SH 6, follow the road to Matakitaki, Upper Matakitaki and the Glenroy Valley road. In places the river lies close to the road; elsewhere it is some distance away. Please ask permission to cross farmland.

LOWER REACHES: From the Matakitaki bridge on SH 6.

☐ Season and restrictions

Open all year below SH 6. Upstream from there, 1 October–30 April. The bag limit is two fish, but above the Glenroy confluence only one may exceed 50 cm.

Upstream from Upper Matakitaki, this medium-sized river is unstable, braided, shingly and flood-prone. Despite the poor trout habitat, there are fish in the more stable pools. However, a lot of walking is required between pools and the river often changes course with floods. There are a few deep, stable holes above Downie Hut, two to three hours' walk from the road end.

The middle reaches are most popular, as the river is much more confined and stable. The bed is rocky and stony and the banks are partially cleared farmland. There are some gorges, but these can be negotiated, especially in low water flows. Some fish on the edges can be spotted but many lie under the shelter of rocky ledges, deep slots and turbulent runs. After rain, the river takes some days to clear. There is a good stock of brown trout averaging 1.4 kg, although much larger fish are also present.

The lower reaches frequently are silt-laden from a west bank tributary entering just upstream from SH 6, and although the river is a bit of a rusher in this section, it is worth fishing. The river is rapidly restocked from the Buller.

MARUIA RIVER

☐ Location

Rises in the Spenser Mountains and flows south through Cannibal Gorge to meet SH 7 near Maruia Springs, close to the Lewis Pass. It then follows SH 7 west to Springs Junction before turning northwest and following SH 65 and the Shenandoah Road. Finally it flows into the Buller River 10 km southwest of Murchison.

☐ Access

There are numerous accesses from SH 65 and side roads including West Bank, Boundary and Creighton roads.

☐ Season and restrictions

Below Maruia Falls the river is open all year, while above the falls the season is 1 October–30 April and the bag limit is two trout.

This long, moderate-sized river is popular and highly recommended as it holds good stocks of medium to large fish in clear mountain water. Drift-dive figures reveal 100 fish per km at Paenga. Along the most fished section of river, between Springs Junction and the Maruia Falls, the banks are lined with native bush, manuka scrub and partially cleared farmland. Here the river is reasonably stable and generally occupies one channel, whereas above Springs Junction it is braided, shingly and unstable.

In the headwaters, including the Alfred River tributary, there are only a few rainbows. Access is from the Lake Daniells track.

Downstream from Springs Junction the majority of trout are browns but there is an occasional rainbow. Fish average around 1.3 kg and can be readily spotted and stalked. The most productive section of river lies in the gorge west of Mt Rutland, where the road leaves the river between Ruffe Creek and the Warwick River confluence. However, it takes a very long day's walk to fish this section.

Below the Maruia Falls there are only browns, and the water is heavier and more difficult to fish with a fly, but there are some good stretches worth exploring.

There are campsites at Maruia Falls, Springs Junction and other locations throughout the valley and most farmers are very helpful when approached. The sandflies can be tough!

LAKE BRUNNER district

More information can be obtained from Greymouth Information Centre

Mail: PO Box 95, Greymouth

Phone: (03) 768-5101

Fax: (03) 768-0317

Email: vingm@minidata.co.nz

Lake Brunner and the small settlement of Moana lie in the central West Coast of the South Island, a 45-minute drive from Greymouth, the main town. On a fine sunny day there is no better place to be on earth than the West Coast. Unfortunately, fine sunny days are few except during February and March, as the annual precipitation can be as high as 3500 mm per year in this area. Despite wet weather and sandflies, the scenery is breathtaking and the brown trout fishing is superb.

Aside from the angling and scenery, the West Coast offers other fascinating diversions. Visit Shantytown and pan for gold, browse through craft shops and jade galleries and, best of all, have a few beers with the locals in a country pub. Your itinerary should also include the Putai Blowhole, Pancake Rocks at Punakaiki, and a drive to South Westland to view the Franz Josef and Fox glaciers. If pressed for time, organise a scenic flight from either Hokitika or Greymouth over Mt Cook and the Southern Alps – it is spectacular on a clear day. A scenic drive over Haast Pass to Wanaka might also be included. In summer, a must for birdwatchers is the white heron colony near Okarito. There are many short walks to take, kayaks to hire and exciting guided rafting adventures to experience.

Scheduled bus services operate from Nelson, Picton and Christchurch and the TranzAlpine train journey from Christchurch to Greymouth via Moana is one of the world's finest. All three routes to the coast by car are stunning: from Nelson via the Buller Gorge, or from Christchurch via the Lewis Pass or Arthurs Pass.

Drop a fly over the reeds.

Heavy brown hooked in Oreti backwater.

Don't let that frisky rainbow run!

Bow and arrow cast.

Bow waves alert fish.

Above:
Brrrr ... southerly coming over the ridge.

Left:
Dappling helps reduce drag.

Right:
Height makes spotting easier.

Below:
Fishing or bridge?

Dry fly or emerger pattern?

So many flies!

Left:
Success on the river edge!

Below:
Fish on at the end of the day.

Accommodation is generally simple but comfortable on the West Coast, with hotels, motels, lodges, farmstays, camping grounds and cabins. There are a few luxury hotels and some of the local restaurants may surprise you.

The Wildfoods Festival in early March is a popular event, offering local fare such as whitebait, wild pork, venison, possum and huhu grubs.

There are sports stores in Westport, Greymouth and Hokitika, but fly-fishing merchandise may be limited. Professional guides are available for hire.

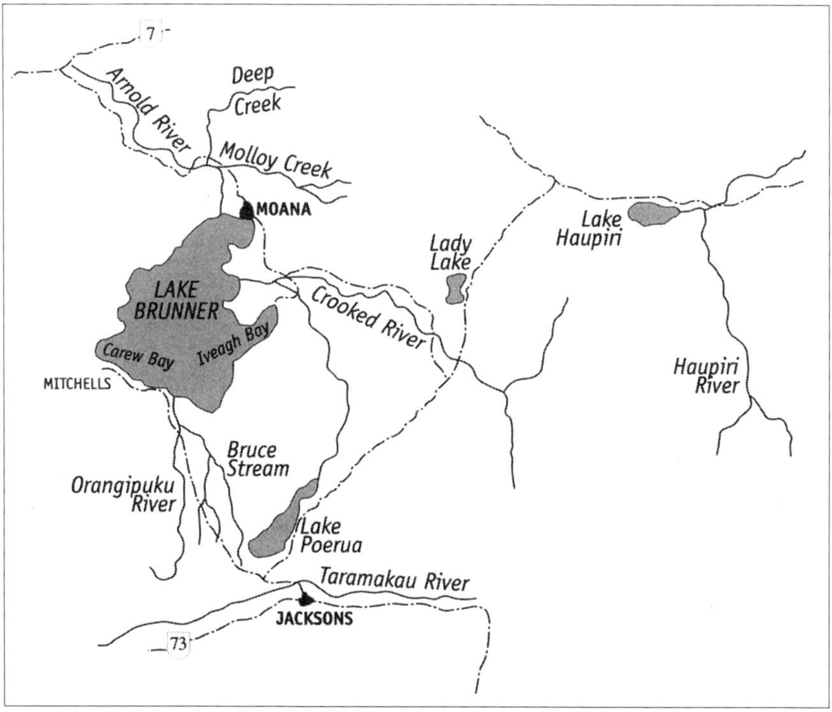

Lake Brunner district

HAUPIRI RIVER

☐ Location

Two branches form the main river. One, a clear snow and rain-fed river, rises near the Harper Pass and flows northwest down a picturesque mountain valley. The other, a heavily tannin-stained tributary, drains Lake Haupiri. The tributaries meet just upstream from the road bridge at the settlement of Kopara to form the main river. This then flows east to join the Ahaura River near the Haupiri farm settlement.

☐ Access

Take the Nelson Creek–Kopara road to Haupiri School. This road crosses the river 1 km past Lake Haupiri and before reaching the school. There is road access from Moana via Bell Hill.

The private Wallace Road follows up the clear-water tributary but permission is required from Gloria Vale Farm Community, phone (03) 738 0224. Alternatively, there is riverbed access from the tributary confluence. Access to the main river, which flows behind the school, is by walking downstream or across private farmland.

☐ Season and restrictions

1 October–30 April. Bag limit is two fish.

In the clear-water tributary, there is 10 km of sight fishing for good-sized brown trout, all the way to the hot springs. The first 2 km of river has been modified by stopbanks but above the farm there are well formed, stable pools. This is boots-and-shorts fishing, with plenty of walking required. The river is easily crossed at the tail of most pools and the grassy banks overhung by bush and scrub provide plenty of terrestrial insects for fish. A farm track makes the return walk easier.

The tributary draining Lake Haupiri is not itself worth fishing, but below the confluence there is excellent water holding very high stocks (200 fish per km). There is easy access to this section of water from the road bridge, with the confluence lying a few hundred metres upstream. Downstream from the road bridge there is excellent water holding plenty of fish, although sight fishing is difficult in the discoloured water.

ARNOLD RIVER

☐ Location

Drains Lake Brunner at Moana and flows north to Stillwater on SH 7 where it enters the Grey River.

☐ Access

There are a number of angler accesses off Arnold Valley Road, some of which are signposted. These include the Moana foot-bridge (at the outlet), Kotuku, Arnold River bridge near Aratika; from Aratika, below the Arnold Dam, Arnold Creek, Old Arnold Road, and Kokiri Bridge (near the freezing works).

☐ Season and restrictions

Open all year; bag limit four sports fish.

This medium-sized, tea-coloured river has been modified by a hydroelectric dam built at Kaimata, 13 km down from Lake Brunner. The water that backs up for 4 km behind the dam is known as Lake Ullstrom. The Arnold River has a very high population of mainly brown trout averaging 1–2 kg (240 fish per km at Kotuku and 75 per km at Kokiri). As the river drains Lake Brunner, it is very stable and remains fishable after rain, especially above Molloy and Deep creeks, although access is more difficult when the river is high. The banks are covered with patches of bush and willows although there are open stretches with gravel beaches, especially when the river is low. Trout can rarely be spotted in the brownish water and the algae-covered stones make wading slippery. The insect life is prolific and at times the fish can become rather selective. There is usually an active evening rise to caddis, when a soft-hackle wet fly, an Elk Hair Caddis or a Goddard Caddis can be most effective. During the day, fish the edges and riffles blind with a small weighted nymph and an attractor-type dry fly as an indicator. In November and December a green beetle imitation works well.

Lake Ullstrom is a series of interconnected willow-lined lagoons which are very difficult to access except by dinghy or float-tube. They contain a good fish population.

Two small tea-coloured streams flowing through farmland, Deep Creek and Molloy Creek join the Arnold at Kotuku, north of Moana. The Arnold Valley Road crosses both creeks near the

Kotuku railway station. These both hold brown trout and are worth exploring, especially early in the season. As with the Arnold, you will need to fish blind because, while some fish can be sighted on a bright day, many more will remain unseen in the discoloured water. There is good road access, but permission should be obtained to cross private farmland.

LAKE BRUNNER

☐ **Location**

At Moana, 25 km southeast of Greymouth.

☐ **Access**

There is limited road access from Moana, Iveagh Bay and from Mitchells at the southern end, but much of the shoreline can be reached only by boat.

☐ **Season and restrictions**

Open all year; the bag limit is four trout.

☐ **Boat launching ramps**

At Moana, Iveagh Bay and Mitchells.

This is the largest lake in the area, some 10 km across. Much of the shoreline, especially on the western side, is bush-covered. The lake holds a large population of brown trout averaging just over 1 kg – a local tourist promotion maintains that most of them die of old age.

Spotting cruising fish is difficult, although a sandy flat near Mitchells and the Crooked and Hohonu deltas can be sight fished. Most blind fly fishing is carried out using a slow-sinking line and a damselfly nymph or bully imitation such as Hamill's Killer, Woolly Bugger or Mrs Simpson. Casting nymphs over weed beds from a boat is also popular, especially near the Bruce River mouth where the trout population is very high.

Trolling a spinner accounts for most of the fish taken, with popular stretches being between Te Kinga Hill and Clematis Bay and near the outlet of the lake. Fish can be caught from the drop-off anywhere in Lake Brunner, with popular spinners being Toby, Cobra and Tasmanian Devil variations.

CROOKED RIVER

☐ Location

Drains the Alexander Range, flows northeast and enters the eastern side of Lake Brunner south of Howitt Point.

☐ Access

LOWER REACHES: 11 km south of Moana, turn off on the road to Iveagh Bay. This road crosses the river. The delta is best accessed by boat.

MIDDLE REACHES: Between Te Kinga and Rotomanu, the road crosses the river. There is easy access both up and downstream. The Bell Hill–Inchbonnie road crosses at the Crooked River Reserve just below a short gorge.

UPPER REACHES: A rough private farm track follows the true left bank upstream to the Evans River confluence. Permission is required from the landowner.

☐ Season and restrictions

1 October–30 April. Bag limit is two trout.

This medium-sized, clear river rises from rugged, inaccessible bushclad mountains. Because of this stability, the river rarely discolours after rain although it becomes more difficult to fish. Frequent floods have cleaned the rock and stone riverbed and made wading and crossing reasonably safe at selected spots. There are well defined, deep pools and runs and although the trout population can be unreliable, the quality of the sight fishing compensates for that.

The upper reaches are partially bushclad, whereas the middle and lower reaches flow across farmland. Trout cannot negotiate the gorge upstream from the Evans River confluence and although the Evans is a spawning tributary, it is an unstable rusher and its fish stocks are very low during most of the year. The middle reaches of the Crooked offer interesting dry-fly and nymph fishing to sighted trout.

BRUCE CREEK

☐ Location

Drains swampy country near the southern end of Lake Poerua, skirts the base of Mt Te Kinga, and together with the Orangipuku River empties into Swan Bay.

☐ Access

From the road junction at Inchbonnie, continue toward Mitchells on the Kumara–Inchbonnie road. Take the northernmost side road on your right, towards Mt Te Kinga. This road reaches the river at an old farm bridge. If you cross the Orangipuku bridge you have gone too far. It is wise to obtain landowner permission even though this is usually a formality.

☐ Season and restrictions

1 October–30 April and the bag limit is two trout.

This slightly tea-coloured spring creek winds its way placidly through partially cleared farmland. Recently, this area has been developed for intensive dairy farming and, with the humping and hollowing method of land development, the Bruce Stream and Lake Brunner are at risk from dairy effluent and fertilizer runoff. The upper and lower reaches are difficult to access because of bush and swamp but the middle reaches offer a full day's fishing. Cross the bridge, walk downstream on the true right bank and fish back upstream. Some fish feeding the edges can be spotted but many will be overlooked unless the water itself is fished. Fish stocks are good and there are some very deep holes. This stable creek remains fishable even after rain. The riverbed is weedy in places, offering a great food supply and shelter for trout. Most fish are caught on a weighted size 14 Pheasant Tail-type nymph but some will rise to a mayfly imitation dry fly during the day.

A few hundred metres above the bridge, the creek divides into three tributaries. The middle tributary is worth following up to where it becomes overgrown. Fish are more easily spotted in the sandy creek bed but are a real challenge to catch.

On favourable evenings there can be a vigorous evening rise and trout emerge from weed beds to feed. However, they can be very selective and frustrating in these conditions. A soft-hackle wet fly fished at a dead drift in the surface film is a good choice.

ORANGIPUKU RIVER

☐ Location

Rises close to the Taramakau River valley, follows the base of the Hohonu Range, joins Bruce Creek just above Lake Brunner and empties into Swan Bay.

☐ Access

The road to Mitchells (Kumara–Inchbonnie road) crosses the lower reaches. A farm track follows down the true right bank almost to the mouth.

☐ Season and restrictions

1 October–30 April. Bag limit is two fish.

Only the 2 km stretch downstream from the bridge and a few hundred metres of water above the bridge are worth fishing. The upper reaches are very overgrown with gorse and scrub, but dairy farm conversion has seen the headwaters diverted into the Taramakau River and the land cleared. This is a small, clear, rain-fed stream where trout can be easily spotted. The river is shingly and as the upper reaches flow across cleared farmland, it rapidly becomes unfishable after heavy rain. The banks are lined with willow, bush, blackberry and gorse, but this also provides cover for anglers spotting fish. Trout numbers are extremely variable – fish seem to move into and out of the lake at will. Fishing is often better late in the season when a spawning run enters the stream. Stealth in stalking and an accurate, gentle presentation are crucial. If another angler is already fishing this stream, it is wise to find an alternative river.

LAKE POERUA

☐ Location

Lies south of Lake Brunner and just north of the Inchbonnie settlement.

☐ Access

From the Inchbonnie–Rotomanu road at Te Kinga Reserve where there are small boat-launching facilities.

☐ **Season and restrictions**

1 October–30 April. Bag limit is four fish.

This small tea-coloured lake holds good numbers of brown trout averaging 1.8 kg. The western side is bush-covered and inaccessible from the shore. There is limited shoreline access north of Te Kinga Reserve and limited access across the swamp at the southern end for hardy, determined anglers. A small boat is a definite advantage as fish can be spotted cruising over mud and sand and can be cast to at a number of locations round the lake. The narrows are a popular spot for trolling and harling. Dead trees and snags can be a problem at the southern end as hooked fish make a beeline for their hide. Cruising fish will accept a small nymph cast well in front of their path.

The next three rivers lie in the Ikamatua, Reefton and Inangahua districts but for convenience are listed in this section. It is one to two hours' drive from Moana to these rivers.

WAITAHU RIVER

☐ **Location**

This major tributary of the Inangahua River drains the Victoria Range, flows northwest and enters the Inangahua 5 km northwest of Reefton. It takes an hour and a half by car from Moana to Reefton via Stillwater and Ikamatua.

☐ **Access**

Gannons Road off SH 69 leads to and crosses the river. Rough 4WD tracks lead upstream on both banks but we suggest leaving your vehicle at the settling ponds on the true left bank and walking. A marked track leads upstream on the true right bank as far as the Montgomerie River confluence (two hours). The Montgomerie Hut offers basic backcountry accommodation up the Montgomerie tributary.

☐ **Season and restrictions**

1 October–30 April. The bag limit is two trout.

This is a small to medium-sized clear bush-lined stream holding browns averaging 2 kg, with a few larger fish in the deeper holes. Numbers are not high but the quality of the angling experience on a sunny day should not be overlooked. The trout become more wary as the season progresses and fish rapidly spook after any wayward or clumsy cast into the gin-clear water. Fishing naturally improves away from the road, with both the Montgomerie River and the upper reaches of the main river well worth exploring. Fishing runs out on the main river at the Shaw Stream confluence, but there is another full day's fishing available on the Montgomerie. The river is normally easy to wade and cross in places, with the granite boulders offering secure footing. The nor'wester blows upstream.

AWARAU RIVER (LARRY'S CREEK)

☐ Location

Flows through heavily bush-covered hills parallel to, but north of, the Waitahu River, to join the Inangahua River 14 km northwest of Reefton.

☐ Access

LOWER REACHES: Crossed by SH 69. You can walk downstream from this bridge or access the river from a picnic area.

MIDDLE AND UPPER REACHES: Turn onto a forestry road up the true right bank. A track follows further upstream from the road end.

☐ Season and restrictions

1 October–30 April. The bag limit is two trout.

This medium-sized river has a reputation for trophy brown trout but they are not easy to entice. They become more selective and difficult after being repeatedly fished over as the season progresses. Although the water is very clear, some of the pools are large and very deep. The fish most commonly accept carefully presented heavily weighted small nymphs, but it can be difficult to get these down deep enough. Larry's Creek is a challenge but the rewards are well worth the effort. There are two to three days' fishing upstream from the bridge. Beyond the Caledonian Pool lies a gorge which can be waded through in low-water conditions. An alternative route to the more open upper reaches is via an old miners' track. Fishing ends at the junction of Farmer and Silcock creeks.

ROUGH RIVER (OTUTUTU)

☐ Location

Rises from the eastern side of the Paparoa Range and flows for 30 km southwest to eventually join the Grey River near Ikamatua.

☐ Access

LOWER REACHES: From Atarau Road, which crosses the river near Ikamatua.

MIDDLE REACHES: From Atarau Road, take Mirfins Road on the true left bank to a sawmill. The sawmill gates close at the end of each working day and at weekends. Anglers can walk upstream across partially cleared farmland and fish to Mirfin Creek. There is also a 4WD track leaving Mirfin Road about 2 km before the sawmill gate. This track takes you up onto a terrace. River access is a steep walk down to the river.

UPPER REACHES: By tramping through untracked bush upstream from Mirfin Creek or flying in by helicopter. The valley has no tracks or huts.

☐ Season and restrictions

1 October–30 April. Bag limit is two fish.

The Rough is very popular with overseas anglers, who usually fly with their guides into the remote bushclad upper reaches between Mirfin and Gordon creeks. However, there is plenty of excellent water downstream from Mirfin Creek. The water is very clear and light greenish, flowing over granite boulders, rock and shingle. Trout can be spotted but many will be missed as they often lie beneath white water or in deep slots in the rock. There are good stocks of browns averaging around 2 kg and these become very spooky later in the season after being fished over. The river can be forded at the tail of most pools as the granite boulders are not slippery.

OMARAMA district

More information can be obtained from Timaru Visitor Information Centre

Mail: PO Box 524, Timaru

Phone: (03) 688-6163

Fax: (03) 688-6162

Email: info@timaru.co.nz

There are also local information centres at Tekapo and Twizel.

Omarama is a small North Otago country town, nestled on the barren tussock plains of the Mackenzie country. It is a centre for gliding in New Zealand and the world championships were held there in 1995. In summer the weather is generally dry and warm but the wind can be problematic. Nearby Lake Ruataniwha is a world-class rowing venue – this is one of a number of lakes created when the Waitaki River was harnessed for hydroelectric power. Lake Benmore is the largest of these lakes to be formed. Other lakes, such as Tekapo, Pukaki and Ohau, are naturally formed but their waters have been diverted for the power schemes.

The surrounding countryside is rather bleak but has great scenic appeal and Mt Cook National Park is less than two hours' drive away. In early December this drive is spectacular because the lupins are in full bloom. Glacial flour in the lakes enhances their colour and beauty and the view through the altar window from the Church of the Good Shepherd at Tekapo has been photographed many times. If time and weather permit, a flight by ski plane from the Hermitage at Mt Cook onto the Tasman Glacier should not be missed. If time is limited, book a scenic alpine flight from Tekapo Airport to view Mt Cook and surrounds.

Accommodation in Omarama includes hotels, motels, and a motor camp, but restaurant facilities are minimal. A small tackle shop is attached to one of the motels but you would be wise to stock up beforehand. A couple working from home in Twizel (30 minutes' drive north on SH 8) tie flies for purchase. Professional trout fishing guides are available for hire for lake fishing on Benmore and fly fishing the surrounding streams and rivers.

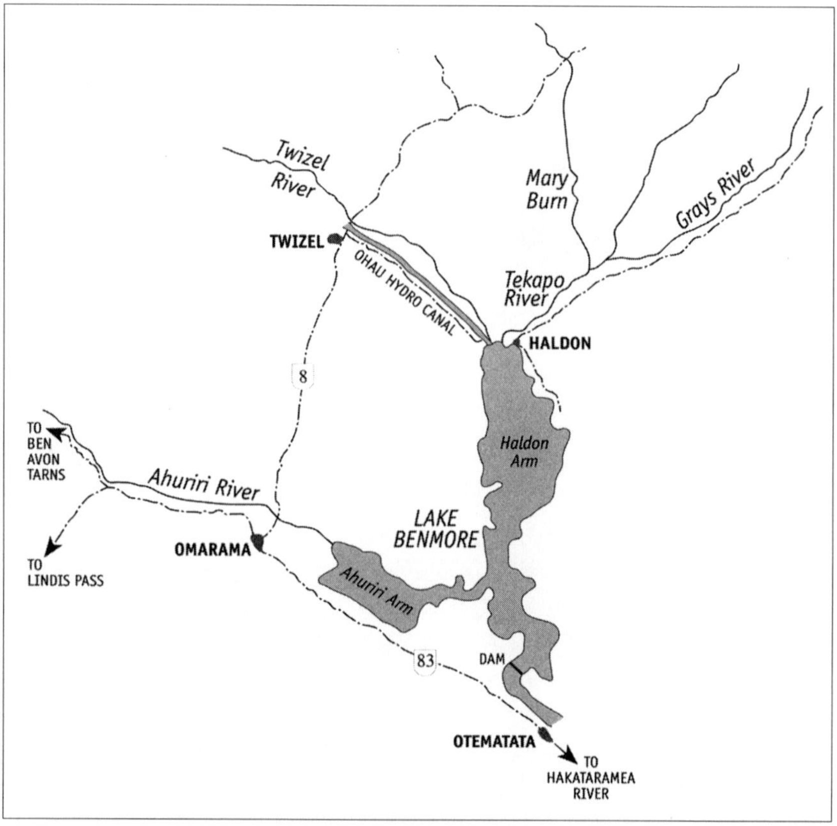

Omarama district

HAKATARAMEA RIVER

☐ Location

Rises near the Hakataramea Pass, flows south and enters the Waitaki River at Hakataramea township opposite Kurow. It is 1 hour's drive from Omarama.

☐ Access

LOWER REACHES: McHenry's Road on the true left or east side of the river follows upstream for 12 km to Wrights Crossing.

MIDDLE AND UPPER REACHES: Above Wrights Crossing access can be obtained from the Hakataramea Valley Road on the west side of the river.

☐ Season and restrictions

First Saturday in November to 30 April. Fly fishing only above the SH 8 bridge. Bag limit is two trout.

This popular medium-sized river offers 30 km of fishable water, although after a dry spring and low water, the trout tend to drop downstream to the Waitaki River. Fish can usually be spotted but some difficult sections should be fished blind as stocks are good. In the lower reaches trout tend to be smaller (140 small to medium-sized fish per km). Upstream in the gorge there are well established pools holding larger rainbow and brown trout. The river can be waded and crossed but the bed of rock and stone can be slippery. In some sections the stream is fringed with willows. The river becomes unfishable when the flow rate is more than 15 cumecs. Salmon spawn in the river late in the season.

LAKE BENMORE

☐ Location

Lies in the Mackenzie country between Twizel, Omarama and Otematata.

☐ Access

AHURIRI ARM (southwestern part, near Omarama): There is walking access from SH 83 to the Ahuriri Delta and lakeshore, 5.5 km from Omarama through Glenburn Station.

HALDON ARM (northern end): Turn off SH 8 at Dog Kennel Corner near Burke Pass and follow the Haldon Road to the camping ground, boat harbour and east side of Haldon Arm. From SH 83 opposite Godley Peaks Road, take the Tekapo Canal road and the Tekapo–Pukaki River road down the true right bank of the Tekapo River from the Tekapo powerhouse to the Iron Bridge and Haldon Arm. A 4WD vehicle is recommended for this rough, shingly road.

WESTERN SHORE: From SH 83 at Ruataniwha Dam, take Falstone Road to the west side of Haldon Arm. From Ohau B powerstation the canal road leads to Haldon Arm and the Ohau River mouth. This mouth can usually be crossed by 4WD vehicle and the Haldon Camp reached after fording the Tekapo River. Extreme care should be taken!

☐ Season and restrictions

Open all year. Bag limit is four trout.

☐ Boat ramps

At Sailors Cutting on Ahuriri Arm and at the Haldon Camping Ground and boat harbour on Grays Road. There are camping sites at Haldon camping ground, Falstone and Sailors Cutting on SH 83.

Formed in 1964, this large, rather inaccessible hydro lake has 116 km of shoreline. Its larger arm, Haldon Arm, tends to hold more milky glacial water from the Tasman Glacier, Lake Pukaki and spillway discharges, while Ahuriri Arm tends to have clearer, snow-fed water. The lake holds a vast stock of brown and rainbow trout averaging 1–2 kg. Sockeye salmon have been liberated in the past but have not done well. Much of the shoreline can only be reached by boat.

Most fish are taken trolling from boats or live-bait fishing with worms. Some hardy anglers use these methods in winter, when snow covers the surrounding mountains.

Both the Ahuriri and Tekapo river deltas offer good 'ambush' fly fishing for cruising trout. The tussock-covered shore on each side of the Ahuriri delta is also a top spot for sight fishing, provided the wind is not strong. Fish will take dry flies, but a small nymph, midge pupa or wet fly cast well ahead of a cruiser is usually more effective.

From the Haldon boat harbour on summer evenings there is good fly fishing from a boat. Trout cruise beneath the willows and will take dry flies such as Coch-y-bondhu, Humpy and Black Gnat.

Access is difficult to many locations without a boat, but much of the shoreline is rather devoid of vegetation and fish. Anglers should concentrate on the locations described, where trout numbers are high.

AHURIRI RIVER

☐ Location

Rises in the Southern Alps below Mt Huxley and between lakes Ohau and Hawea. Flows on a curving easterly course down the Ahuriri Valley to enter Lake Benmore near Omarama.

☐ Access

THE DELTA: There is an angler access from SH 83 through Glenburn Station, 5.5 km from Omarama. It is a 20-minute walk to the delta.

LOWER REACHES: Walk downstream from the SH 8 bridge. There is vehicle access through Ben Omar Station but a fee is charged.

MIDDLE REACHES: SH 8 runs parallel to the true right bank of the river from Omarama to Dunstan Downs Station. Be sure to get permission from Killermont Station for walking access to the river. Access to the true left bank is from Quail Burn Road and the branch road to the Clay Cliffs.

UPPER REACHES: Beyond Dunstan Downs Station, 17 km south of Omarama, take the gravel Birchwood Road to Ben Avon and Birchwood stations. This follows upstream for 25 km, although the river is often some distance from the road. Permission must be obtained before walking across private farmland on Ben Avon or Birchwood stations. The river can also be reached by walking down Avon Burn.

☐ Season

Above Longslip Creek, the Ahuriri and tributaries open on the first Saturday in December and close on 30 April. Below Longslip

Creek, 1 October–30 April. The bag limit above Longslip Creek is two trout. Below this creek, four trout.

This medium to large-sized river has a reputation for trophy fish in its upper reaches and is protected by a water conservation order. Over recent years angling pressure, especially from overseas visitors, has made it more difficult to secure a stretch of unfished water. The river winds across pastoral land in a very exposed valley and the prevailing nor'wester can make upstream angling impossible by 10 am. There are long, slow, deep glides where some fish can be spotted on a bright, still day. However, others remain hidden under banks and only emerge to feed at dusk. In the Native Cutting section on Ben Avon Station, the river comes to life. There are well developed stable deep pools and runs over a rocky and stony riverbed. Some trout along the edges can be stalked but many remain hidden in the rocky crevices and deep holes. Stocks are not large in the upper reaches but most fish are well worth catching. Both rainbow and brown trout average over 2 kg in the upper reaches, with some browns over 4 kg. Weighted nymphs account for many of the fish caught but in high summer, cicada and grasshopper imitations can provide brilliant fishing. The river can be crossed in places, in low-water conditions only. Above Birchwood Station, fish are few and far between as the riverbed of fine silt and sand is usually on the move.

The middle reaches below Longslip Creek are more swift, unstable and braided, but still hold good stocks of browns and rainbows that can be sight fished in ideal conditions. Many of the rainbows are small in this section but the browns average 1–2 kg. This section is not subject to the same angling pressure as the upper reaches and often provides a good alternative. Trout can be taken on a lure fished downstream, but most of them will be small rainbows.

Below SH 8 bridge the river braids through willows but stocks of fish averaging 1 kg are high (90 trout per km).

This snow and glacier-fed river can flood in alarming fashion with nor'westerly storms and remain unfishable for three or four days at a time. It is best fished when the river flow is well below 29 cumecs and on hot, windless summer days.

AHURIRI VALLEY LAGOONS

☐ Location and access

These lagoons are accessible from the right side of Birchwood Road 2 km north of Ben Avon Station. Although the present Ben Avon runholder is happy for responsible anglers to fish, it is polite to gain prior approval. The lagoon on the left side of the road is private.

☐ Season and restrictions

First Saturday in December to 30 April. Fly fishing only. Bag limit is two trout.

These lagoons, Ben Avon, Horseshoe, Watson and Yellow, are old oxbows of the Ahuriri River cut off after floods. Most have some connection with the main river, and they can become silt-laden when the Ahuriri River is in high flood. Their shores are swampy tussock dotted with a few willows and the soft silt lake beds are dangerous to wade. Large browns cruise the weed beds and these can keep you interested all day in relatively calm and bright conditions. They are very difficult to stalk and deceive. A long fine tippet is required, with the fly cast well ahead of cruising fish. Just when you think the fish is on track towards your fly, it turns and goes the other way. Try small unweighted nymphs and emergers or even a small damselfly. In February, a cicada imitation either scares the fish or induces a smash-and-grab take.

GRAYS RIVER

☐ Location

Drains swampy country near Burke Pass, flows south across the Mackenzie Plains, around the western foot of Grays Hills and into the Tekapo River.

☐ Access

Turn off SH 8 on to Haldon Road, at Dog Kennel Corner west of Burke Pass. This road follows the true left bank of Grays River, albeit some distance away, and eventually reaches Haldon Arm of Lake Benmore.

LOWER REACHES: From Haldon Arm camping ground, follow up the true left bank of the Tekapo River, past Iron Bridge. After a long bumpy ride this rough gravel road eventually fords the Grays River on a series of concrete posts. We recommend a 4WD vehicle.

MIDDLE AND UPPER REACHES: There are two marked angler accesses off Haldon Road, one opposite the Mackenzie Pass Road, and a number of private vehicle tracks to the river. Permission is required from local landowners to use the tracks that are not clearly marked 'Angler Access'.

☐ Season and restrictions

First Saturday in November to 30 April. Bag limit is two trout.

This small to medium-sized spring creek holds a good stock of brown trout, with a few rainbows in the lower reaches. Most fish are 1–2 kg but there are larger fish present. The lower reaches are choked by willows but upstream beyond the willows there can be excellent sight fishing. Sometimes, especially early in the season when the river is full, trout can be difficult to spot. For this reason it is also worth fishing likely-looking water. The river has a sand, gravel, weed and mud bottom and the banks are grassy between willows, with some swampy sections. Where there are no willows, glare on the water can also make spotting difficult and you will inevitably spook fish. There are some deep corner holes and hides beneath banks and the river is very stable. Best in calm, sunny conditions when the trout are rising. The more sheltered stretches can be fished in a nor'wester and there are 20 km of fishable water. If a vehicle is already parked at your chosen site, find another section of river. Be mindful: it is heavily fished.

TEKAPO RIVER

☐ Location

Drains Lake Tekapo via control gates and flows south to enter Haldon Arm on Lake Benmore. The upper river has been severely modified for hydroelectric power generation and there is very little worthwhile fishing above Forks Stream.

Access

Most roads and tracks along the Tekapo River are very rough and a 4WD vehicle is recommended.

LOWER REACHES: From Ohau B powerstation on SH 8, take the canal road to the Ohau River crossing just above the mouth. If this stretch of water is low, then it can be forded and the Tekapo River reached by vehicle.

Haldon Road leaves SH 8 at Dog Kennel Corner and leads to the Haldon Camping Ground. Drive through the camp to the river.

MIDDLE REACHES: Rough gravel roads run along both banks with side tracks through the willows to the river. Iron Bridge provides a crossing point about 2–3 km above Lake Benmore, if the approaches haven't been washed out by winter floods. Turn off SH 8, 1.5 km south of Tekapo township opposite Godley Peaks Road onto the Tekapo Canal Road. Cross the canal and continue on a rough gravel road down the true right bank of the Tekapo River. This road runs for 35 km and joins up with roads that go upstream. There are many access tracks off this road.

Season and restrictions

Below the lower power pylons 1 km upstream from the mouth, the river is open all year. Above these pylons, from the first Saturday in November to 30 April. Bag limit is four trout.

Although this medium-sized river is subject to fluctuating flow rates as a result of power generation, it holds very high numbers of trout (250 trout per km). It has a mean residual flow of 12 cumecs but becomes unfishable when the Tekapo spillway is fully open.

The riverbed is wide, shingly, somewhat unstable and exposed to the nor'wester. On a sunny day in spring when the orange Californian poppies are in flower there is no better sight than looking upstream toward snow-covered Mt Cook. The river is heavily willowed in some sections and braided in others. Wading is not difficult and the tails of most pools can be crossed. There are long, deep glides and ripply, shallow runs. Trout can be spotted along the edges in optimal conditions but you will miss many fish unless you fish it blind. After heavy rain, the river dirties from silt brought down by Forks Stream. It may take three days to clear.

The larger fish often lie deep beneath the drop-off at the head of the deeper pools, where only heavily weighted nymphs or a mouse imitation at night will interest them. The majority of fish are browns but some good-conditioned rainbows in the lower reaches can be exciting. Trout will respond to a wide selection of flies and lures, although during a rise they can be selective. This is an ideal river for beginners with plenty of fish, plenty of safe water and few casting obstructions. However, beware of the nor'wester.

There are a number of side channels and ponds in the Tekapo Valley and most contain trout. Pattersons Ponds below the Tekapo spillway hold some good-sized browns.

TWIZEL RIVER

☐ Location

Drains the Ben Ohau Range, flows generally south through the outskirts of Twizel and across the Mackenzie Plain to enter the Haldon Arm of Lake Benmore.

☐ Access

UPPER REACHES: From SH 8 take Rhoboro Station Road, which crosses the river.

MIDDLE REACHES: Where SH 8 crosses at Twizel. A private farm road follows down the true right bank; permission required. There is also access across farmland from the continuation of the road to the black stilt research centre.

LOWER REACHES: By walking access upstream from the Ohau River crossing near the mouth.

☐ Season and restrictions

First Saturday in November to 30 April. Bag limit is two trout.

The middle and lower reaches of this small freestone stream offer 20 km of sight fishing for browns averaging 1–2 kg. Avoid nor'westerly conditions as the wind blows downstream and there is no shelter apart from an occasional willow. The upper reaches are flood-prone and unstable but are worth a look early in the season, as is the Fraser tributary reached from the Glen Lyon Road west of Twizel.

MARY BURN

☐ Location

The upper reaches flow south, parallel to the eastern shoreline of Lake Pukaki. The middle reaches are crossed by SH 8, then wind across flat Mackenzie country pastoral land before entering the Tekapo River in the Grays Hills area.

☐ Access

MIDDLE REACHES: From SH 8, although permission must be obtained from local runholders on Mary Burn and Simons Hills stations.

LOWER REACHES: The Tekapo–Pukaki canal road crosses the lower reaches, where there is a sheltered campsite.

☐ Season and restrictions

First Saturday in November to 30 April. Bag limit is two trout.

This small exposed stable shingly stream has been heavily fished in recent seasons. Holds mainly brown trout but early in the season rainbows add some 'spice'. There are good stocks of fish averaging 2 kg that can be stalked on a bright, sunny day. It is impossible to fish in strong nor'westerly conditions, and on cloudy days sight fishing is very difficult owing to glare on the water. The stream is easily crossed and the banks of grass, briar rose and matagouri scrub do not greatly impede casting. The lower reaches near the campsite are choked with willows. Trout rise avidly to dry flies presented without drag and will just as avidly accept small weighted nymphs. There is two days' worth of fishing from the campsite to SH 8.

WANAKA district

For more information contact
Wanaka Visitor Information Centre

Mail: PO Box 147, Wanaka 9192
Phone: (03) 443-1233
Fax: (03) 443-1290
Email: info@lakewanaka.co.nz

The small, rapidly growing holiday and retirement township of Wanaka lies on the shores of beautiful Lake Wanaka in West Otago. This is a haven for outdoor activities, with hunting, aerobatic and scenic flights, guided tramping, horse trekking, jetboating, kayaking, mountaineering, paragliding, rock climbing and rafting. In winter a number of ski fields are open.

Other attractions include the biennial Warbirds over Wanaka air show, the New Zealand Fighter Pilots' Museum, a wide range of tours, an enormous maze, and wine tasting at Rippon Vineyard on the shore of the lake. An hour's drive south to Cromwell takes wine enthusiasts to a wide variety of exciting vineyards. The town also offers two small local galleries and a pottery, a library, a good golf course and many picnic and barbecue areas.

There is a wide choice of accommodation, including camping grounds, motorhome sites, cabins, backpackers, bed and breakfasts, homestays, farmstays, motels, hotels and resorts. Some interesting cafés and restaurants add to the local flavour. It is approximately six hours' drive from Christchurch and four and a half hours from Dunedin.

You would be wise to fill your fly boxes in Christchurch or Dunedin, although some fishing gear can be purchased in the township. A number of professional fishing guides are available for fly fishing or boat fishing on the lakes.

LAKE WANAKA

☐ Access

Road access to this large lake is somewhat limited and some of the best fishing spots can be reached only by boat. The Glendhu Bay Road generally follows within walking distance of the shore while the road to West Wanaka offers access to Paddock Bay. SH 6 follows the eastern shore from the head of the lake to The Neck. Aubrey, Beacon Point, Maungawera and Dublin Bay roads give limited access near Wanaka township.

☐ Season and restrictions

The lake is open to fishing all year. Bag limit is six sports fish. Fishing is prohibited within 150 m of the launch wharf and within 100 m of the marina wharf. Bait fishing is prohibited.

☐ Boat launching

From Wanaka marina, Glendhu Bay and Camp, Waterfall and Wharf streams up the eastern side of the lake.

Lake Wanaka is a large, scenic lake in an old glacial valley. It holds an enormous resource of fish including brown and rainbow trout and land-locked quinnat salmon. Trolling is a popular method of fishing throughout the year, although in winter it can be very cold. Popular spots are the river deltas including the Matukituki and the Makarora, the bluffs at Hell's Gate, and Stevensons Arm. Spinning from the shore is productive except on a bright, calm summer's day. Lead lines and outriggers are legal.

There is plenty of scope for shoreline fly fishing in summer, as the water is clear and trout can be ambushed cruising the drop-off and shallows. Small lightly weighted nymphs, soft-hackle wet flies, damsel imitations and a Black and Peacock snail pattern are effective on cruisers that are feeding below the surface. Suggested dry flies include Humpy, Coch-y-bondhu, Black Gnat, Green Beetle and Royal Wulff.

In the colder months of the year, browns cruise the shallows after spawning and will take bully-type lures such as Woolly Bugger, Mrs Simpson, Hamill's Killer and Rabbit patterns. Dublin Bay and Stevensons Arm are popular for this type of fishing.

The weed and sand flats at Paddock Bay, West Wanaka, are a favourite spot to intercept cruising trout. Small lightly weighted nymphs, Black and Peacock or soft-hackle flies are cast well in front of cruising fish and twitched when a fish approaches. Careful, slow wading, plenty of patience and good spotting conditions are critical.

Good fish can be caught at the Makarora and Matukituki deltas late in the season using a smelt fly and a high-density sinking line.

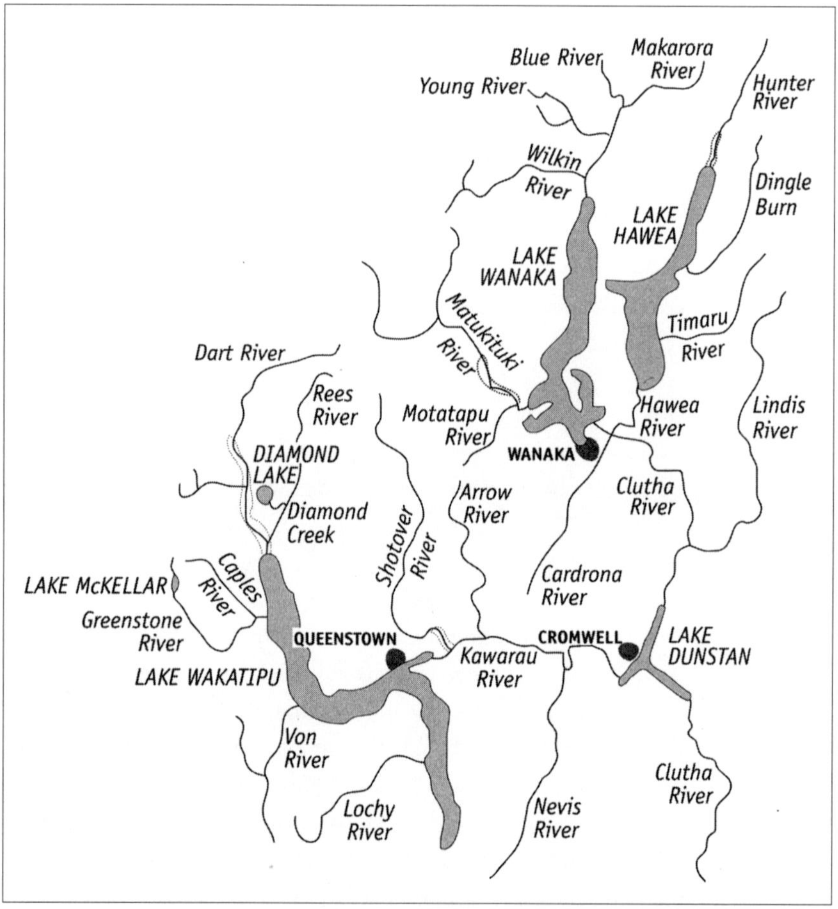

Wanaka and Queenstown districts

WILKIN RIVER

☐ Location

The headwaters saddle with the East Branch of the Matukituki River and drain the alps of the Mt Aspiring National Park. The main river flows generally east, to join the Makarora River 9 km above the head of Lake Wanaka.

☐ Access

The Makarora River usually needs to be forded upstream of the confluence, only possible in low-water summer conditions. Then the Wilkin River itself must also be crossed about 2 km upstream from the confluence. Both these fords can be dangerous because of soft silt and strong currents. Tramper anglers should first check river conditions at the Makarora Store or at the DoC office.

A jetboat service operates from Makarora village and can carry trampers and anglers to within 2 km of Kerin Forks Hut. Bookings can be made from a kiosk near the Makarora Store. You can also fly into a bush airstrip at Kerin Forks, where there is a DoC hut with 10 bunks, which is heavily used by trampers.

☐ Season and restrictions

1 November–31 May. Bag limit is one trout.

This medium-sized river can carry snowmelt and glacial flour until Christmas. As it drains a large alpine catchment, the river rises rapidly in heavy rain and readily discolours. The lower reaches are unstable and often silt-laden and generally not worth fishing. The best water lies at Kerin Forks, 16 km upstream from the Makarora confluence. Here the pools are more stable and rocky, the water is clear and the fish stocks are reasonable, especially early and late in the season. The majority are rainbows, with a spawning run from Lake Wanaka late in the season, but the occasional brown up to 4 kg has been caught. Sight fishing is possible on some stretches but the deeper pools and runs should not be bypassed without casting a fly. There is a day's fishing above Kerin Forks, up to a steep gorge. The valley is exceptionally beautiful with dense beech bush and grassy clearings overhung by sheer snow-capped peaks. Take insect repellent for the sandflies.

The tributary streams, Siberia and Newland, offer small-stream fishing in their lower reaches only.

YOUNG RIVER

☐ **Location**

Flows parallel to, but north of, the Wilkin River and enters the Makarora River 4 km downstream from the Blue River confluence.

☐ **Access**

From SH 6 north of Makarora village look for the access track at Brady's Creek. This leads across farmland to the Young–Makarora confluence. The Makarora River must then be forded. This is difficult unless all the rivers are running reasonably low. At times the best crossing can be either upstream or downstream from the confluence. The tramping track follows up the true left bank.

☐ **Season and restrictions**

1 November–31 May. Bag limit is one trout.

This beautiful small mountain river is now heavily fished, especially by commercial operators. It has deteriorated over the past 20 years but is well worth visiting for its scenic qualities alone and there is always the chance of catching a nice rainbow. There are few fish in the lower 2 km and, in the gorge section, there are usually a few scattered fish, very easy to spot from the access track but often difficult to reach. The best fishing lies just below the forks, two to three hours from the Makarora confluence. Here, there are some pleasant, stable pools holding rainbow averaging 1–2 kg.

There is also good fishing up the north branch for 1 km before a formidable gorge blocks progress; there are no fish in the south branch. The trout are not fussy and, as with most sight fishing in the back country, stalking, presentation and an accurate first cast are all-important. The fish become spooky as the season progresses. Try attractor dry flies, weighted nymphs or even lures swung down and across. There are good campsites at the forks clearing and the valley is popular for tramping. Take sandfly repellent.

LAKE HAWEA

Access

SH 6 follows the western shore from the outlet near Hawea to The Neck. A branch road continues to the DoC camping ground at Kidd's Bush and beyond to Hunter Valley Station. The road to Timaru Creek follows the eastern shore. Four kilometres beyond Timaru Creek, the road to Dingle Burn Station becomes private and permission should be obtained before travelling further up the lake.

Season and restrictions

The lake is open all year. Bag limit is six fish.

Boat launching

At Hawea Motor Camp, from SH 6, from a beach at The Neck and from Hunter Valley Station.

This lake suffers from fluctuating levels as a result of hydroelectric power generation. There is still good shoreline fishing, although it is best when the lake level is low. There are good stocks of brown and rainbow trout, and land-locked quinnat salmon which are usually caught by trolling spinners from a boat. Hot spots for shoreline anglers are The Neck, the delta of Timaru Creek and adjacent shore, and the mouths of Dingle Burn and Hunter rivers. The latter are best accessed by boat although it is a long trip to the head of the lake only to find a nor'wester roaring down the Hunter Valley. Trout are easy to spot and ambush on a bright day. Favourite dry flies include Coch-y-bondhu, Black Gnat, Humpy, Royal Wulff and Parachute Adams. Any small weighted nymph is usually acceptable, as are lures such as Mrs Simpson, Monsum's Bully, Hamill's Killer, Yellow Dorothy and other smelt imitations.

HUNTER RIVER

☐ Location

Rises from the Bealey Range on the Main Divide near the source of the Wills River. From the forks in the headwaters, the main stream flows south for 30 km before entering Lake Hawea.

☐ Access

By boat to the top of Lake Hawea. Through Hunter Valley Station by 4WD vehicle (permission required).

By helicopter or fixed-wing aircraft. There are two airstrips in the valley.

It is a 16-hour tramp from Hunter Valley Station to Forbes Hut.

☐ Season and restrictions

1 November–31 May. Bag limit is one trout.

This is a large snow and glacier-fed river flowing down a wide, picturesque but exposed valley. The nor'wester frequently ends any chance of upstream fly fishing. Trout are difficult to spot as the water usually carries some glacial flour but stocks are sufficient to warrant fishing the water. It is best fished when low during February and March, especially when the cicadas are chirping. The river is swift and difficult to cross but there are long, deep runs and stable pools sufficient to entice any angler. Holds mainly rainbow trout averaging 1.5 kg, with a few good browns for variety.

Around the mouth, backwaters and side channels are all worth exploring, along with a small spring creek nearby. Lure fishing with a smelt imitation across and down stream can be very productive. Spinning also accounts for many trout caught.

From Long Flat Creek (Ferguson Hut) to the forks (Forbes Hut), the river is usually confined to one channel and there is excellent fly water. In summer when the river is low, it is hard to go past a cicada imitation such as a Stimulator, large Humpy or Irresistible. The river rises rapidly with rain in the headwaters and can take three or more days to clear and return to normal. Despite being rather inaccessible, this river is worth a visit especially on a calm, bright summer's day but such days are all too infrequent in this valley.

DINGLE BURN

☐ Location

Drains mountains on the northeast side of Lake Hawea, flows southwest and enters the lake north of Silver Island.

☐ Access

HEADWATERS AND UPPER REACHES: By fixed-wing aircraft or helicopter. By tramping over a saddle from Birchwood Station in the Ahuriri Valley. There is a horse track to follow for some of the way on the three-hour journey. Permission required from Birchwood Station. By tramping upstream from the mouth and through the gorge (six hours) with many river crossings.

MIDDLE REACHES: The gorge can be reached either from above or by walking upstream from the mouth.

Lower reaches and mouth: By boat, or by private road through Dingle Burn Station. Permission is required and the road is extremely narrow and tortuous.

☐ Season and restrictions

1 November–31 May. Bag limit is one trout.

The best water lies in the upper reaches where this small mountain stream rushes down a wide tussock valley lined with beech bush. Unfortunately, over recent years, guides and their clients have overfished the stream. Some of the rainbow trout can be spotted but many will be missed in the fast-flowing, bubbly runs. It pays to fish this pocket water blind. Fish average 1–2 kg, but their condition is often below par, especially after they have been caught and released a few times. Most will accept weighted nymphs and attractor-type dry flies, provided you cast short to avoid drag. A landing net is very useful.

The gorge always holds a few trout in stable, deep pools and most of these can be sight fished. Many of the pools are short and eliminating drag is a essential for success. It is only fishable in low water during summer.

The lower reaches between the gorge and the mouth are braided and unstable and hold very few fish.

At the mouth, the shallow shoreline close by always presents a few cruising fish that can be stalked.

CLUTHA RIVER (UPPER REACHES)

☐ Location

Drains Lake Wanaka and flows south to Lake Dunstan.

☐ Access

There are many access points but some of the main ones are from Beacon Point Road off Dublin Bay Road; from SH 6 and SH 8A at Albert Town and Luggate; Deans Bank from Alison Avenue at Albert Town; and from Maori Point Road.

In places, private farmland needs to be crossed so please ask permission. The Upper Clutha Angling Club has published an excellent pamphlet detailing all the accesses to the upper Clutha River and Lake Dunstan. These are available from local sports stores.

Before fishing at night it is worth exploring the access and looking at the river. In some places, a steep cliff needs to be negotiated before the river can be reached and this might prove difficult in the dark.

☐ Season and restrictions

Deans Bank, 1 October–31 May. This section of river is marked by two posts, one near the outlet of Lake Wanaka and the other 600 m above the Albert Town bridge.

Elsewhere, the Upper Clutha is open all year. Deans Bank is reserved for fly fishing only. Above the Luggate Bridge, fly and artificial bait only. Bag limit is six fish.

☐ Boat ramps

Boats can be launched from the outlet, Albert Town bridge and Luggate.

This very large river has the highest flow rate of any New Zealand river, making it difficult to fish. As it drains a lake, the upper reaches are stable and remain clear even after heavy rain, although fishing becomes challenging when Lake Wanaka is high. Drift diving has established that, near the outlet, this river holds the highest biomass of fish of any New Zealand river, with 275 fish per km.

During the day, many large trout lie sheltered behind boulders in deep, fast water where it is nearly impossible to get your fly or spinner down to them. At night, some of these fish move into the edges of the current and over weed beds and shallows to feed, becoming more accessible to anglers. Wading is safe, provided you avoid the strong current. Both rainbow and browns, some over 5 kg, occupy this magnificent waterway and, with the strong current, anglers fishing during the evening and at night would be well advised to use strong tippets and have at least 100 m of backing. Trout are virtually impossible to spot but rise freely at dusk in favourable weather, especially to caddis. The best months for this type of fishing are December to the end of February. Fish feeding on caddis usually exhibit a splashy type of rise, as caddis emergers leave the water in great haste. Frequently, this caddis rise does not begin until late at night. If you are fortunate enough to strike a good caddis rise, try a floating line and cast a deer-hair or Goddard Caddis, or even a soft-hackle wet fly across and downstream and swing the fly through the rising fish. Hang on! The take can be explosive.

During the day, try fishing any shallow run or weed bed with weighted nymphs, or dry flies such as Humpy, Royal Wulff, Coch-y-bondhu, Black Gnat, Irresistible or Parachute Adams. Rainbows especially will also take lures such as Woolly Bugger, Rabbit patterns, Parson's Glory or Mrs Simpson fished on a sinking or shooting-head line. At night, a large black Hairy Dog or similar lure on a sinking line can produce a few surprises. Long casts and a powerful rod are an advantage for this type of water.

Spinning accounts for many fish and, again, long casting is required to adequately cover the water.

The stretch of water upstream from Lake Dunstan is braided and more easily reached by boat. However, there is some excellent fishing beneath the willows and late in the season there is a good spawning run of fish. These can be fished 'Taupo-style' with lures such as Red Setter and Orange Rabbit on a heavy sinking line or weighted nymphs and egg patterns on a floating line.

LAKE DUNSTAN

☐ Location

This large hydro lake was formed in 1993 following the construction of the Clyde Dam on the Clutha River.

☐ Access

There are three arms to the lake – the Clutha, Kawarau and Dunstan – but the Clutha arm is by far the most productive fishery. SH 6 follows its western shore from Cromwell towards Wanaka, and the 'Angler Access' signs off this highway are marked. SH 8 follows the eastern shore of Clutha Arm from Cromwell until it bends east to Tarras.

Access to the less favoured Kawarau arm is from SH 6 to Queenstown and the bridge to Bannockburn, but a boat is a great advantage.

Dunstan Arm is also best accessed from a boat, although SH 8 follows its northeastern shore from Cromwell to Clyde.

☐ Season and restrictions

Open all year. Bag limit is six fish.

Initially this lake was a very productive fishery but a severe flood in 1994 covered the weed beds with silt and destroyed much of the insect life. The lake has now recovered and good fishing can be expected, especially round the Clutha River delta and the weed beds at the top of the Clutha arm. Both brown and rainbow average 1.4 kg and small landlocked quinnat salmon add some interest, especially for trollers. Most fish are caught from boats either trolling or harling a fly but there is some good sight fishing available from the shore. Spinning from the shore can also be worthwhile although after Christmas the weed beds are problematic. For the fly angler try Midge Pupa, Corixa, Damsel nymphs, Black and Peacock, Green Beetle, Willow Grub and, in January and February, terrestrial patterns such as cicada and cricket imitations. Mrs Simpson, Hamill's Killer and other bully-type lures can also attract fish. A float-tube or dinghy is most useful and enables you to fish the holes and open areas between the weed beds.

QUEENSTOWN district

For additional information contact Queenstown Visitor Information Centre

Mail: PO Box 353, Queenstown

Phone: (03) 442 4100

Fax: (03) 442 8907

Email: qvc@xtra.co.nz

Queenstown, on the shores of Lake Wakatipu, has one of the most spectacular settings in the world. This world-famous tourist destination is renowned for its clear mountain air and long summer twilights. Take note, however, that mountain weather is very changeable and rapid turns are not uncommon. New Zealand airlines provide scheduled daily flights return from Auckland, Rotorua, Wellington, and Christchurch. It is a six to seven-hour drive from Christchurch and four to five hours from Dunedin.

Queenstown's great outdoors offers a year-round playground. In winter it is a major ski resort and, in the warmer months, aside from the scenic attractions, the thrillseeker can bungy jump, tandem parapente, hang-glide or parachute, and jetboat or raft the whitewater of the Shotover and Dart rivers. For a more peaceful and serene time, there are many attractive local walks. The more energetic can tramp in the scenic Routeburn, Greenstone or Dart valleys.

There is a selection of shops, malls, restaurants, bars and nightclubs that cater to every age, taste, and budget and, for those wishing to gamble, there are casinos.

In January, for a look at a New Zealand lifestyle, the Lake County Agricultural and Pastoral Show and the Glenorchy Races present a wonderful display of New Zealand country living and farming. The Wine, Food and Jazz Festival, also held during January, is a delightful break from a day's fishing. A lake cruise and visit to Walter Peak

Station on the historic steamer *Earnslaw*, or a ride on the gondola, offer superb views of the lake and the Remarkables. Golfers will enjoy the Millbrook course near Lake Hayes, designed by Bob Charles. Train buffs might be interested in a short ride on the historic *Kingston Flyer*, and for the wine connoisseur there are a number of boutique wineries in the Kawarau Gorge. For additional 'retail therapy' or lunch, a stop in historic Arrowtown should not be missed.

Accommodation is not a problem, provided it is booked well in advance, and the range is broad, from backpackers' hostels to luxury first-class hotels.

Fishing gear may be bought in city centre sports shops but the discerning angler would be well advised to stock up on specialist equipment in Christchurch or Dunedin. Local professional fly fishing guides are available for hire. If your itinerary does not allow time for a day's fishing in this area, feeding the tame trout off the Queenstown wharf may suffice.

LOCHY RIVER

☐ Location

Rises in the Eyre Mountains and follows a northeast course to enter Lake Wakatipu at Halfway Bay.

☐ Access

This is difficult, and most overseas anglers hire a helicopter and a guide. To the lower reaches by boat to the mouth and walking upstream. To the headwaters, by tramping over mountainous country from the Mt Nicholas Road; to the middle and upper reaches, by 4WD vehicle on private roads from Mt Nicholas and Cecil Peak Stations.

Before camping in the area, permission should be obtained from Halfway Bay, Cecil Peak, Walter Peak and Mt Nicholas Stations. The Long Burn hut has six bunks and is open to the public.

☐ Season and restrictions

1 November–31 May. Fly fishing only; the river is open for fishing only below the Billy Creek confluence. Only one fish may be taken.

The Lochy is an excellent medium-sized mountain river offering more than 15 km of sight fishing for mainly rainbow trout averaging 1.5 kg. Like the Greenstone and the Von rivers close by, the Lochy is an important spawning river for Lake Wakatipu. Although this river holds resident trout, 60 percent of fish will have returned to the lake by Christmas.

The lower reaches flow across developed farmland and become braided at times but there are plenty of fish, especially early in the season.

Upriver from the Long Burn the river enters a gorge with native bush lining the river in some sections. Here the river is more turbulent, but excellent fishing is available to active anglers prepared to scramble over rocks and ford the river. This section is best fished in boots and shorts. A tramping track follows up the true right bank.

Above the gorge, the river valley opens out again and fishing is much easier. There is excellent water all the way upstream to Billy Creek. As fish are easy to spot in stable pools and runs, this section is heavily fished by overseas anglers and their guides.

Trout are rarely selective when recovering from spawning and will accept a wide variety of dry flies and nymphs presented without drag. Try Humpy, Stimulator, Coch-y-bondhu, Green Beetle, Royal Wulff, Dad's Favourite and Irresistible dry flies. Nymphs: Green Stonefly, Perla and Hare and Copper.

The mouth offers lure fishing for running fish late in the season and smelt fly fishing in summer.

VON RIVER

☐ Location

The north branch drains the Thomson Mountains while the south branch drains the Eyre Mountains. From the branch confluence in the upper reaches, the river flows north to enter the western shore of Lake Wakatipu just north of Whites Bay and Mt Nicholas Station.

☐ Access

By boat to the mouth and lower reaches. From Mt Nicholas Road via Mavora Lakes. This road follows down the true right bank almost to the mouth.

☐ **Season and restrictions**
1 November–31 May. Bag limit is one trout. Fly fishing only.

This small to medium-sized mountain stream is a highly regarded rainbow trout fishery. It is a spawning river for Lake Wakatipu and although it holds fish throughout the year, many spawning fish in the upper reaches will have returned to the lake by Christmas. The south branch enters a steep gorge which can only be fished by active anglers in low-water conditions. Once in the gorge, there is no way out until you reach the end. Below the north branch confluence, the river flows through tussock grassland for 15 km before entering the lower gorge. This ends about 2 km upstream from the mouth. The lower gorge is very difficult to access and fishing is also possible only when the river is low. Early in the season, some mending fish will be in poor condition but most are hungry and not very selective. Trout are easy to spot in very clear water and will take many varieties of well presented dry fly and nymph. Fish average around 1.5 kg. The upper gorge is sheltered and can be fished in westerly winds. The river rises rapidly with rain and becomes dirty, taking three or four days to clear.

The mouth fishes well in April and May, especially with sunk lures and smelt imitations.

GREENSTONE AND CAPLES RIVERS

☐ **Location**
Drain the Livingstone, Ailsa and Humboldt mountains and Lake McKellar. The Caples River flows south and joins the Greenstone 6 km from its mouth. Together, they enter the western side of Lake Wakatipu north of Elfin Bay.

☐ **Access**
A rough gravel road from Kinloch leads to a carpark 3 km up the Greenstone from its mouth. From here anglers can walk upstream on a walking track to both rivers.

There is a three-hour walk from the Divide carpark on SH 94 (Te Anau–Milford road) to the McKellar Hut on the upper reaches of the Greenstone River. The track is well defined but steep in parts. Overseas anglers often hire a helicopter and a guide.

☐ Season and restrictions

1 November–31 May. Bag limit is one trout. Fly fishing only.

The Greenstone is a medium-sized spawning river for Lake Wakatipu but the middle and upper reaches are easily waded and crossed. The Caples is smaller, and both have very clear mountain water, enabling sight fishing. Both valleys are very scenic, with bubbling rivers winding across wide tussock flats fringed with beech bush and overhung by snowy mountains. Tramping is very popular, especially in summer and the DoC huts are often fully booked. Both rivers are heavily fished, especially by overseas anglers and their guides.

As with the Von River, many of the rainbows in the upper reaches of the Greenstone River return to the lake by Christmas. The most productive and easiest water to fish, especially early in the season, lies upstream from the Pass Burn, the route to Mararoa Saddle. The main obstacle to fishing is the westerly that blows straight down both valleys. Fish are easy to spot and stalk and are unselective as far as fly patterns are concerned. However, they are readily spooked, especially after having been fished over a few times. Wear drab colours and adopt the usual stalking techniques. Remember, an accurate first cast is very important. Rainbows average 1.4 kg, with the odd brown usually larger. Before Christmas, fish stocks are excellent, walking and casting are easy and the river is safe to cross and wade.

Below the Pass Burn, the river becomes more difficult to fish, with rocky gorges and fast runs; but for active, agile anglers, it is well worth a look for resident fish.

Below the Caples confluence, the river is considerably larger. The mouth offers good lure fishing, especially late in the season when trout gather near the delta before their spawning run.

The Caples holds slightly larger fish than the Greenstone and not all are easy to spot. When spotting is difficult, it pays to blind-fish the likely-looking turbulent water. An access track follows up the true left bank until it crosses at a swingbridge. Use similar flies as listed for the Lochy River.

ROUTEBURN RIVER

☐ **Location**

Drains the Humboldt Mountains and joins the true right bank of the Dart River opposite Paradise, at the head of Lake Wakatipu.

☐ **Access**

Only the lower reaches are worth fishing, as the river goes underground. Take the Routeburn Road from Kinloch and turn off to the carpark for Lake Sylvan. Upstream from the swingbridge there is access to only a few pools. Below this bridge there is good water right down to the Dart confluence.

☐ **Season and restrictions**

1 November–31 May. Catch and release. Fly fishing only.

This small short clear rocky and stony tributary of the Dart holds a few good-sized brown and rainbow trout and is heavily fished. Fish are usually easy to spot but become extremely wary as the season progresses.

DIAMOND LAKE

☐ **Location**

Lies 15 km north of Glenorchy on the road to Paradise.

☐ **Access**

The road follows the eastern shore, enabling easy walking access to the eastern and northern shores. The western shore is heavily bushclad and steep.

☐ **Season and restrictions**

Open all year. Bag limit is three trout. Fishing from a mechanically powered boat is permitted.

This small, clear, scenic lake holds a good stock of brown trout averaging 1.2 kg. When the weather is calm and sunny, these can be stalked and ambushed along the shoreline and in the shallow bays. Unweighted nymphs, Black and Peacock, Midge Pupa and Damselfly are all good patterns to try. For rising fish try Parachute Adams, Black Gnat and Coch-y-bondhu dry flies.

DIAMOND CREEK

☐ Location

Drains Diamond and Reid lakes and flows south for 4 km before entering the Rees River.

☐ Access

There are two marked angler accesses. One is from Paradise Road and the other is near the Priory Road bridge.

☐ Season and restrictions

1 October–31 May. Bag limit is one fish. Artificial bait and fly only.

This medium-sized stream resembles a spring creek with stable undercut tussock banks, native bush and a weedy stream bed. Normally it is clear but after strong winds the lakes become rough and the discoloured water can affect the stream. There are reasonable numbers of good-sized browns and rainbows sufficient to tempt any angler but these become very shy and well educated as the season progresses. Careful stalking, small mayfly and caddis imitations and an accurate presentation are required. As is usually the case at the head of Lake Wakatipu, the nor'wester can play havoc with fishing this stream.

GORE district

For further information contact
Gore Information Centre

Mail: PO Box 1, Hokonui Heritage Village, Norfolk St, Gore

Phone: (03) 208 9908

Fax: (03) 208-9908

Email: goreinfo@esi.co.nz

Gore, in eastern Southland, occupies a strategic position in the southern tourist angler's circuit, with roads radiating west to Fiordland, south to Invercargill and east to the rugged Catlins Coast. The excellence of its brown trout fishing has given Southland a world reputation and Gore claims to be the 'brown trout capital of the world'. Gore is a moderate-sized country town serving a wealthy farming community, one hour by car from Invercargill, two and a half hours from Dunedin and one and a half hours from Te Anau.

On non-fishing days we suggest visiting Invercargill and the Southland Museum to see live tuataras; attending Tulip International in the spring or early summer, taking a vintage aircraft flight from Mandeville or seeing the porcelain dolls at the Dollsmiths in Mataura. If golf is on the agenda there are courses in Gore, Mataura and Invercargill.

Accommodation is adequate, with motels, hotels, homestays and camping grounds. In this area we would suggest a farmstay to better acquaint yourself with the local customs.

Fishing guides are available for hire in Gore as well as in Balfour (30 minutes' drive). Sports shops have adequate supplies of fishing equipment.

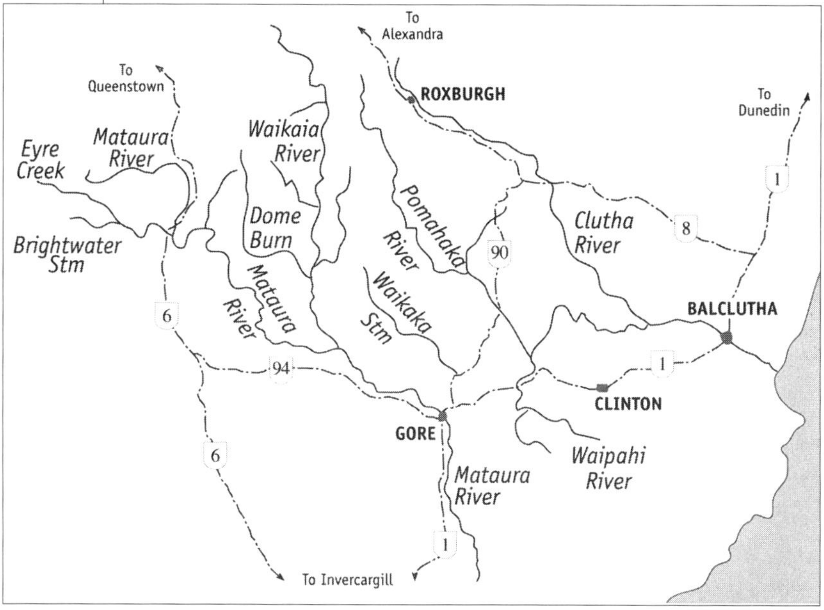

Gore district

MATAURA

River and tributaries

MATAURA RIVER

☐ Location

Rises in the Eyre and Garvie mountains south of Lake Wakatipu, flows southeast to Gore and then south to enter the sea at Fortrose.

☐ Season and restrictions

Open all year below the Gorge Road bridge on SH 92. Above this bridge, 1 October–30 April.

Above the Garston bridge, one fish of less than 40 cm may be taken. Below the Garston bridge, four trout may be taken.

Fishing from boats, float-tubes or other flotation devices is permitted only below Mataura Island bridge.

For descriptive purposes, this famous trout fishing river, providing over 150 km of fishable water, is divided into three sections.

Upper Mataura (Fairlight to Cattle Flat)

☐ Access

There is access from SH 6 just north of Garston from a bridge that crosses the river and Hume Road. Cainaird Road off SH 6 at Fairlight offers access to the headwaters. Downstream from Parawa, a gravel road running east follows down the river into the Nokomai Gorge.

There are additional access tracks across private farmland from SH 6, but permission is required from local landowners.

The upper Mataura River runs over a gravel bed and is willow-lined. Brown trout of 1–2 kg are relatively easy to spot under normal conditions and fish stocks are good (40 fish per km at Nokomai; 40 percent of these are a good size). They become more spooky as the season progresses and accurate casting to sighted fish is essential for success. The upper river is quite small and can be crossed at the tail of most pools. There are deep holes beneath willows, long glides and shallow riffles. Between Nokomai and Cattle Flat the river runs through a gorge but this is, as a rule, easy to negotiate and fish. It can be walked in one long day but it is better fished over two or three days. Early in the season the river usually contains snowmelt but by mid November it runs clear and the river recovers reasonably rapidly after rain.

Mayflies and caddis predominate and nymphs, emergers, soft-hackle wets and dry flies all take fish. We suggest trying Pheasant Tail and Hare's Ear nymphs, CDC emergers, Dad's Favourite, Twilight Beauty, Parachute Adams, March Brown, Dark Red Spinner, Kakahi Queen and Elk Hair Caddis dry flies and Purple Grouse soft-hackle wet flies. Later in summer, Willow Grub and some terrestrials can be useful.

Middle reaches (Cattle Flat down to Gore)

☐ Access

There are numerous access points with some being the Ardlussa–Cattle Flat road, Ardlussa Bridge, Waipounamu Bridge, Pyramid Bridge at Riversdale, Mandeville, Otamita Bridge, Monaghans Beach at Croydon and Graham's Island on the east bank at Gore.

This is the most popular stretch of river, although the water quality has deteriorated and sight fishing is no longer an option.

Overseas anglers enjoy this section because the water itself must be fished – unless, of course, trout are rising. Matching the hatch can be crucial. The riverbed is still predominantly gravel, the mudbanks are covered with grass and willows and this stretch supports a healthy stock of browns averaging about 1 kg; however, there is the occasional fish up to 4 kg. Above the Waikaia confluence the river can be waded and crossed in normal conditions, but below the confluence the river swells to the point where crossings become more hazardous. Trout are often more selective from this point downstream and there are some interesting backwaters to explore, some of which remain clear when the main river is dirty.

Use the same flies as described for the upper Mataura, plus Midge Pupa and Corixa, especially in the backwaters. During the 'mad Mataura rise' try a small unweighted dark-bodied nymph or a soft-hackle wet fished at a dead drift. Use a small indicator or even a small Parachute Adams that is easily visible. When the trout are unresponsive, it may be worth inspecting the river to determine the food source, and subsequently operating on a fly with a pair of scissors to match the hatch!

Lower reaches (Gore to the mouth)

☐ Access

SH 1 more or less follows the river from Gore to Edenvale on the west, true right bank. However, there is easier access from the east or true left bank, especially between Mataura and Gore. Further downstream there are numerous roads near Tuturau, Wyndham and Seaward Downs, with SH 92 crossing on Gorge Bridge at the top of the tidal section.

The best water lies upstream from Mataura Island, as below this point the river becomes channelled and unattractive and the river is much larger and deeper, with an occasional coal reef altering the character of the riverbed. There are long glides and willows with a substantial population of trout present. Some of these are large and often difficult to catch. Again use mayfly, caddis, Midge Pupa and Corixa imitations, and a Black and Peacock to imitate snails. Spin and livebait anglers enjoy good success in these lower reaches, especially when whitebait are running.

WAIKAIA RIVER

☐ Location

Rises in the Umbrella Mountains just east of the Pomohaka River headwaters. Flows south for 50 km, first through native bush and then pastoral land before joining the Mataura River at Riversdale.

☐ Access

The Riversdale–Waikaia–Piano Flat road and side roads offer generally easy access to the river. Beyond Piano Flat, the Whitcombe Road leads to Whitcombe Flat but leaves the river. This is a 4WD road that can be negotiated in dry weather by conventional vehicles, but the trip is worthwhile only for its scenic qualities. The Waikaia River track follows upstream from Piano Flat closer than this road and provides better access. There is pleasant, basic camping at Piano Flat, but carry insect repellent.

☐ Season and restrictions

1 October–30 April. Bag limit is four trout. Boats, float-tubes and pontoon boats are not permitted on this river.

This moderate-sized highly regarded brown trout river is the Mataura River's major tributary. The rugged, bushclad, inaccessible headwaters upstream from Piano Flat hold few trout. At Piano Flat there is interesting, slightly tea-coloured water offering sight fishing in bright conditions. Fish stocks are good (40 trout per km) and the river can be waded and crossed in places. Once the river emerges from the bush and crosses farmland, sight fishing becomes more difficult and you have to look for rising fish or fish feeding along the edges of runs. The banks are clay and mud with willows and grass. There are long glides, deep pools and shallow riffles. Fish average 1–2 kg, and the same selection of flies as described for the Mataura River is effective.

OTAMITA STREAM

☐ Location

Rises in the Hokonui Hills, flows east and joins the Mataura River just downstream from the Waimea Stream/Mataura River confluence at Mandeville.

☐ Access

Lower reaches, from behind Mandeville village on the Otapiri–Mandeville road south of Mandeville. Middle and upper reaches, from the Otapiri–Mandeville, Otamita Valley and Glenislay roads.

☐ Season and restrictions

1 October–30 April. Bag limit is four trout below the Otamita Gorge road bridge and two above.

This pleasant, small stream flows over a rock and gravel bed. In the lower reaches, willows line the banks but the middle and upper reaches have a stable riparian margin of tussock with some flax. The banks are generally open for flycasting, although lumpy tussock can impede progress in the top section. The water is slightly tea-coloured, so most fish are caught blind fishing with small weighted nymphs and dry flies, but some trout can be spotted. In summer larger terrestials are worth trying, especially in the middle and upper reaches, while Willow Grub can be effective in the lower sections. A reasonable stock of browns in the 1–2 kg range are present, with fewer but larger fish in the upper reaches. Carry a landing net.

POMOHAKA RIVER

☐ **Location**

This long river, protected by a water conservation order, rises in the Umbrella Mountains south of Roxburgh and winds its way for 125 km through West Otago farmland to enter the Clutha River below Clydevale, not far from the mouth of the Waiwera River. Because the river is so long, it is divided into three sections here.

☐ **Season and restrictions**

1 October–30 April. Bag limit above Park Hill Bridge is three trout. Below this bridge, the limit is six.

Upper reaches above Switzers Bridge

☐ **Access**

From the following roads running northeast of Heriot, Kelso and Tapanui: Aitcheson's Runs Road to Hamiltons Flat and the headwaters; Switzers Road to Park Hill Domain; Hukarere Station Road, and Spylaw Burn Road.

The headwaters run deep in a rocky gorge lined with beech forest. Access is tricky and river crossings can be hazardous. The country above the gorge is barren and windswept and can be very cold, even in February. Only fit anglers should attempt this section, as you need to be like a mountain goat. Large sea-run browns up to 5 kg, which run upstream from the Clutha to spawn from January to March, are the attraction of this river. By mid April, most fish have paired up for spawning and they become unresponsive to anglers. There are stable, deep holes and fish can be spotted but are wary, so must be approached with finesse.

From Hamilton Flat to Switzers Bridge, the river runs through tussock and grazing country. The river is easy in this section and can be safely waded and crossed. The water is clear and fish can be spotted on a rock, stone and gravel bed. They respond to carefully presented weighted nymphs, especially stonefly and caddis varieties, and to cicada, Black Gnat, Coch-y-bondhu and small mayfly imitations.

Middle reaches (Switzers Bridge to Conical Hill)

☐ Access

From Dusky Forest, Kelso township, Paradise Flat Road, Tapanui–Waikaka bridge, Gore–Tapanui bridge, Waipehi–Conical road and Waikoikoi Road.

Trout are smaller in this section and average around 1.2 kg but stocks are good. The water becomes brownish in colour and sight fishing is hardly an option. There is a variety of water, some of which is overgrown with willows. The best stretch is in Dusky Forest, where the river rushes through on a slippery rocky and stony bed. Wading and crossing can be treacherous but blind nymph and dry-fly fishing can be exciting. Carry a landing net for this section. Below Dusky Forest, the river slows and is heavily willowed but between Kelso and Tapanui another gorge offers additional challenging fishing.

Lower reaches from Conical Hill to the mouth

☐ Access

Many roads offer access but some sections of the river are significantly overgrown with willows and impossible to fish. Burkes Ford, Ross and Taumata roads along with the Clinton–Clydevale and the Waiwera–Clydevale roads lead to or cross the river.

Below Conical Hill, the water becomes even more peat-stained and the river more choked with willows. There are swift, rocky runs and deep guts, with spinning the best option for this section. Below Burkes Ford, the river slows, deepens and becomes more muddy and weedy. Most fish in this section are caught on live bait. The mouth can be accessed on foot from Swans Bridge, across private land.

The size and number of resident trout in this popular river have diminished over recent years. Even the run of sea-run fish is considerably less than a few years ago. Water abstraction and farm pollution are thought to be the cause.

WAIPAHI RIVER

☐ Location

Rises from swampy country west of Clinton and winds its way north across open, swampy farmland to join the Pomohaka River south of Conical Hill.

☐ Access

LOWER REACHES: SH 1 crosses the river near Arthurton 20 km east of Gore.

MIDDLE REACHES: Jeffs Road off the Clinton–Mataura road crosses the river.

UPPER REACHES: The Clinton–Mataura back road crosses the river, while the road to Wyndham follows upstream. The best stretches of river are reached through private farmland.

☐ Season and restrictions

1 October–30 April. Bag limit is six trout.

There is more than 35 km of fishable water on this small stream, which hosts the Waipahi Gold Medal competition in late October each year. The stream is tannin-stained from its swampy origins so sight fishing is generally impossible unless fish are rising. Although reasonably small, this river has some deep holes and rocky runs and brown trout stocks are excellent. Fish average around 1 kg. There are prolific hatches on this river especially early in the season and trout can be very selective. Best fished either early or late in the season as low water in summer heralds the onset of weed growth.

Small mayfly nymphs, emergers, No-Hackle Duns and mayfly dry flies account for most fish taken. Caddis patterns can be useful at dusk.

Other streams worth fishing in the Gore area include the Otapiri, Waimea and Mimihau.

Spotting the edges of the Ahuriri River.

Otamita River.

Above:

Keep a low profile.

Left:

Dull colours provide good camouflage for stalking.

Right:
Precision casting necessary.

Below:
River access can be risky.

Whitestone River reward.

Lower Waiau River.

Hook-up on the Eglinton River.

Mararoa River.

Spectacular Mackenzie Country vista.

Spotting the Wilkin River.

Bruce Creek.

Trout on!

South Mavora Lake.

North Mavora Lake.

TE ANAU and iordland district

More information can be obtained from Real Journeys Visitor Centre, Lakefront, Te Anau

Mail: PO Box 1, Te Anau

Freephone: 0800 656501

Fax: (03) 249-7022

Email: info@realjourneys.co.nz

Web: www.realjourneys.co.nz

The hub of Fiordland is the small tourist town of Te Anau, nestled on the edge of Lake Te Anau. Fiordland National Park is a World Heritage Park and every day during summer many busloads of tourists pass through Te Anau en route to Milford Sound or to walk the Milford Track, touted as the most beautiful walk in the world. As Te Anau lies on the edge of Fiordland, its rainfall is considerably less than the 6000–8000 mm per year that parts of Fiordland experience. However, the weather can be cool and unsettled, especially in the spring. February and March are the warmest and driest months.

Fiordland National Park offers scenery that is unsurpassed – snow-capped mountains, dense native bush, shimmering lakes, sheer rock walls, cascading waterfalls and deep fiords. A scenic flight over this area on a clear day is an unforgettable experience, as is a boat trip on Milford or Doubtful Sound or to the head of Lake Te Anau. Other scenic sensations include the glowworm caves, the newly developed underwater observatory in Milford Sound, the underground Manapouri powerhouse (on the west arm of Lake Manapouri), and a drive up the Eglinton Valley to Milford via the Homer Tunnel. In January, you can even see horse racing in the main street of Te Anau. Golfers will enjoy the Te Anau course along the shores of the lake. There are tours of all descriptions, from nature, photography and ecology holidays to guided walks and tramps. The Kepler, Milford, Greenstone, Routeburn and Hollyford tracks will satisfy any lover of glorious wilderness country.

We advise you to call DoC or the Real Journeys Visitor Centre in either Queenstown or Te Anau for additional details and weather updates.

Accommodation caters to every budget and it is wise to book ahead in this tourist resort. Although Te Anau is a small town there are a considerable number of restaurants that will please the most discerning palate.

The sports shop in town has an adequate supply of fly fishing tackle and there are a number of professional fly fishing guides available for hire.

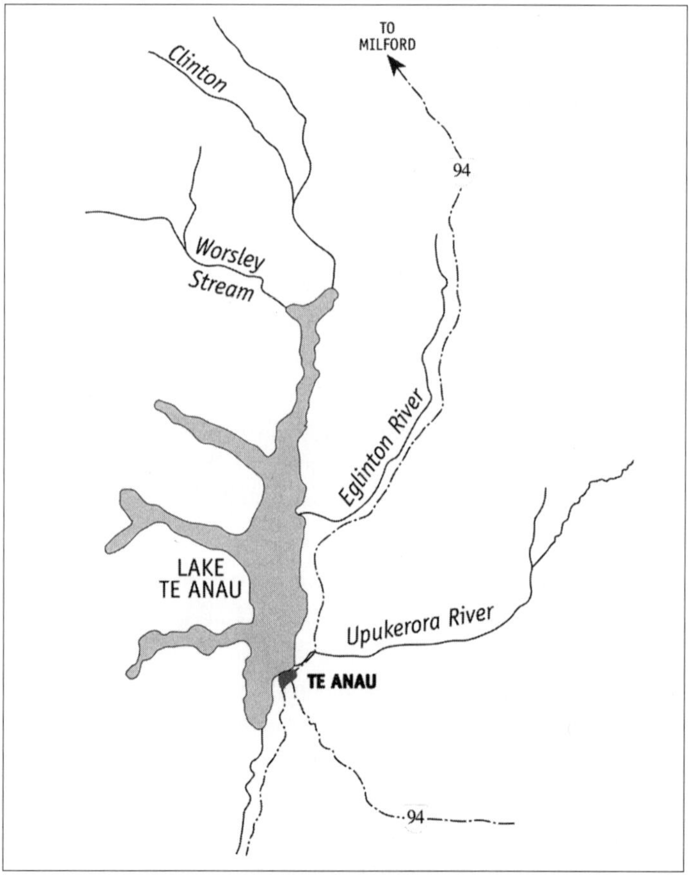

Te Anau district

LAKE TE ANAU

☐ Location

Between Fiordland National Park and the Eyre and Livingstone mountains of South Otago. The western shore is broken up into fiords that penetrate deep into the rugged bush-covered Fiordland mountains.

☐ Access

Limited road access along parts of the eastern shore; elsewhere by boat, floatplane or by tramping.

☐ Season and restrictions

Open all year. Bag limit is four trout.

This is the largest lake in the South Island – it is 61 km long, 417 m deep and covers 850 ha. The eastern shore is drier; it is covered in grass and scrub and is farmed.

The lake is best fished by trolling from a boat or spinning from the shore, although there are a few spots, mainly at stream mouths, where fly anglers can fish. Fish are hard to see except at shallow deltas such as the Eglinton. There is good shoreline fishing at the golf course and in nor'wester conditions trout can be seen cruising in the waves. Night lure fishing at stream mouths can be excellent. The lake contains rainbow and brown trout along with a few landlocked Atlantic salmon. The lake level is controlled at the outlet by a weir.

There are a number of clear mountain streams well worth fishing on the western side of Lake Te Anau, with access by boat or floatplane. All the streams drain steep, heavily bushed country and anglers need to combine tramping with angling. The streams include the Glaisnock (at the head of the North Fiord), the Lugar Burn (also entering the North Fiord), Doon River (on the southwest arm of the Middle Fiord) and the Ettrick Burn, which enters the lake just north of the Te Anau Glowworm Caves.

CLINTON RIVER

☐ Location

Rises near the McKinnon Pass on the Milford Track, flows south-east and enters the head of Lake Te Anau near Glade House.

☐ Access

By boat from Te Anau Downs to Glade House and the start of the Milford Track. The track follows up the true right bank to Mintaro Hut. By tramping a very difficult route over Dore Pass from the Eglinton Valley – this trip is for experienced trampers only.

Camping is permitted only away from the Milford Track, and permission must be obtained from DoC, Te Anau. At times there may be accommodation available at Glade House.

☐ Season and restrictions

1 November–31 May. Bag limit is two trout. Artificial bait and fly only.

This magnificent moderate-sized clear mountain river holds good numbers of brown and rainbow trout up to 4.5 kg. Fish are easy to spot but careful stalking and an accurate first cast are crucial. Use a long, fine trace but of sufficient strength to hold large fighting fish stripping off 50 m of line with their first run. The river is rocky and stony, with bush overhanging the water in places. Crossings are tricky and deeper than they appear, because the water is very clear. With heavy rain the river will rise rapidly but, as the headwaters drain dense bush, the water seldom becomes silt-laden. It may become tannin-stained for a few days, but it rapidly recovers. Most trout, when hooked, seek the shelter of a hide beneath sunken logs and flood debris, so landing them is a real challenge. Trout will accept small weighted mayfly and caddis nymph varieties, and dry flies such as Coch-y-bondhu, Humpy, Royal Wulff, Irresistible, Elk Hair Caddis and Parachute Adams can bring results. Careful stalking, accurate casting and a drag-free presentation are generally more important than the fly pattern. Don't forget insect repellent – the sandflies are a bother!

The North Branch, Neale Burn and Lake Ross all hold good-sized trout for experienced tramper anglers who are unafraid of torrential rain and sandflies. Lake Mintaro, which was formed by a landslide, also holds a few good fish.

WORSLEY STREAM

☐ **Location**

Drains Lakes Sumor and Brownlee, flows east and enters Lake Te Anau at Worsley Arm.

☐ **Access**

By boat or floatplane from Te Anau.

☐ **Season and restrictions**

1 November–31 May. Bag limit is two trout.

This remote medium-sized scenic river flows through rugged bush-covered mountainous terrain, the habitat of wapiti (see Glossary p 202), and holds browns and rainbows up to 4 kg. The river is rocky and stony and can be forded in places, provided the river level is normal. Most trout can be spotted but all likely-looking water should be fished.

The lower reaches are deep and difficult to access except by boat, and the track upstream on the true left bank is rather overgrown and washed out in some sections. The Park Board hut along the beach from the mouth is heavily used, especially on weekends and holidays in summer.

The middle and upper reaches offer stable pools and sparkling runs, and good fishing is available to beyond the Castle River confluence for those willing to explore.

The Castle River itself holds a few large rainbows in deep clear pools and these are a real challenge to hook. Use the same flies and methods as outlined for the Clinton River.

EGLINTON RIVER

☐ **Location**

Flows into and out of Lakes Fergus and Gunn, then south down the scenic Eglinton Valley to enter Lake Te Anau north of Te Anau Downs.

☐ **Access**

SH 94 follows the river upstream on the true left bank, although a walk across tussock flats and through beech bush may be necessary to reach the river. The mouth can be accessed from a 4 km-long gravel road leaving SH 94 at Te Anau Downs.

☐ Season and restrictions

1 November–31 May. Fly fishing only. Bag limit is two trout. Fishing from any flotation device is not permitted.

This moderate-sized freestone river offers over 30 km of fishing, with reasonably easy access from the main road. It is a spawning river for Lake Te Anau but also holds resident fish. Rainbow and brown trout averaging around 2 kg are present in good numbers and most of these can be sight fished in bright, clear conditions. The river can take three or four days to clear after heavy rain and often carries snow and glacial melt early in the season. However, it fishes best early in the season during periods of low water flow. In normal conditions it is safe to wade and cross at the tail of most pools. The riverbed is shingly and the banks covered in grass, scrub and patches of beech bush.

The most productive water lies between Walker and Mackay creeks and below Knob's Flat, although trout are present up as far as Cascade Creek. There are large fish in the gorge but this is virtually inaccessible. Fish are not selective and will respond to a variety of carefully presented weighted nymphs and dry flies. Although some trout can be sight fished, test all good water.

There are a number of small side creeks of the Eglinton River that hold fish early in the season. The East Branch is fast-flowing and unstable in the lower reaches but active anglers can find better water three hours' tramp upstream. The access track is marked near the road bridge.

UPUKERORA RIVER

☐ Location

Rises in the Livingstone Mountains, flows southwest through patches of bush, scrub and pastoral land and enters Lake Te Anau at Patience Bay just north of Te Anau township.

☐ Access

MOUTH: From the south side of Upukerora bridge on SH 94, take Upukerora Road then gravel tracks to the mouth.

LOWER REACHES: SH 94 crosses the river 3 km north of Te Anau. Walk upstream from the bridge.

MIDDLE REACHES: Five kilometres south of Te Anau, turn off SH 94 onto Kakapo Road and then onto Ladies Mile Road or Dale Road. Look for the 'Angler Access' signs.

UPPER REACHES: From the end of Kakapo Road through private farmland. Permission must be obtained.

☐ Season and restrictions

1 November–31 May. Bag limit is two trout.

This long medium-sized freestone river is also an important spawning stream for Lake Te Anau. Holds mainly rainbow trout averaging 1 kg, and larger browns are present in the upper reaches. Although close to Te Anau township, the river holds good stocks of fish, many of which cannot be spotted in the fast runs. It is well worth fishing all likely-looking water as well as sight fishing the edges of runs and pools. The nor'wester tends to blow upstream and this can be a real bonus. The river is easy to wade and cross and is a great learner stream.

Provided the mouth is not too braided, there is good lure fishing at night.

WAIAU RIVER

☐ Location

This large river drained Lake Manapouri before the Mararoa Weir was built below the Mararoa confluence. Now this water is held back in the lake for hydroelectricity generation at West Arm on Lake Manapouri. Below the weir, the river flows south close by Monowai and Clifden to eventually reach the Te Waewae Lagoon south of Tuatapere.

Upper Waiau River (Te Anau to Manapouri)

☐ Access

From Te Anau township, Golf Course Road leads to the weir and the outlet. The Kepler Track follows down the true right bank.

From the Te Anau–Manapouri road there are a number of

access points. The two most popular are Queens Reach and Rainbow Reach. There is a basic camping area at Queens Reach and boat-launching facilities.

☐ Season and restrictions

1 October–31 May. Bag limit is four trout. Boats are permitted for access.

This large, heavy, deep, clear river holds a good stock of rainbow and brown trout but shoreline access is very difficult because of overhanging manuka scrub and beech trees. The lower 3 km of river upstream from Lake Manapouri are unstable, contain fallen trees and are unattractive to fish. A boat is a great advantage for access and the river fishes best when the water level is low. When the control gates are open and the river is high, most shingle banks and islands are covered with water, and the river can only be fished in a few spots with spinning gear. In low-water summer conditions, excellent blind fly fishing with dry flies and nymphs can be enjoyed.

Rainbows around 1–2 kg are most commonly caught and these fight extremely well. Fish can rise during the day and evening and night sedge fishing can be spectacular. Recommended shoreline fishing spots include the control gates, the boat ramp, Rainbow Reach, Balloon Loop and the Kepler Track. Use mayfly and caddis imitations and attractor patterns.

The mouth at Lake Manapouri is a favoured spot but a boat is necessary as wading is treacherous in soft silt.

Lower Waiau River (below Mararoa Weir)

☐ Access

MOUTH AND LOWER REACHES: SH 96 crosses at Tuatapere and at Clifden. Roads follow down both banks from Tuatapere with the Tuatapere–Riverton road offering access to the lagoon on the eastern side just south of Te Waewae settlement. King's Island below the Clifden Bridge can be accessed only through private property.

MIDDLE REACHES: Between Clifden and Redcliff there are a number of access points, many through private property. Most property owners readily give permission but please ask before fishing. Some access points are:

- Motu Bush Road, off Lill Burn Valley Road on the west side of the river, across private farmland.
- Wairaki River mouth, reached by a track on the south side of the Wairaki bridge.
- From Glendearg Station north of the Wairaki River.
- From Sunnyside Station on the west bank south from Monowai.
- From Monowai powerstation and the Borland Burn mouth north of the powerstation, both on the west side of the river.
- From Blackmount Station.
- From Redcliff Station from a road leaving the top of Redcliff Saddle.

UPPER REACHES: From Whare Creek on Jericho Station; from Excelsior Creek.

☐ Season and restrictions

Open all year below Tuatapere bridge, including Te Waewae Lagoon (excludes the Holly Burn). Above this bridge and upstream to the Mararoa Weir, 1 October–31 May. Bag limit is four fish. Boats and other flotation devices are not permitted between the Mararoa Weir and the Monowai River confluence. Fishing is not permitted within 100 m of the fish pass in the Mararoa Weir.

This once large and magnificent river has been severely modified for hydroelectric power generation. However, water flows have recently been increased to not less than 12 cumecs and this has dramatically improved the fishing. Unfortunately, silt builds up periodically in the Mararoa Weir and flushing this downriver adversely affects the trout and aquatic life. The river holds brown and rainbow trout with an occasional large sea-run brown entering the lower reaches. Fish up to 4.5 kg can be anticipated, although most of those caught are 1–2 kg.

At the mouth, in the lagoon and upstream to Tuatapere, most trout are caught on live bait or spinners, especially when whitebait are running. The Kings Island area south of Clifden is popular early in the season but access is difficult when the river is high, because of riverbank vegetation.

Between Clifden and the Wairaki mouth access is easier – the river is more spread out and the banks are lower. Fish cannot be spotted, so all likely-looking water should be covered. Above the

Monowai powerstation, rainbows become the predominant fish and the river, although large, is more stable and confined to one channel.

There is good water downstream from Whare Creek, with good numbers of well conditioned rainbows in the 1–2 kg range. Again, trout are difficult to spot but will rise to dry flies. In normal conditions the river can be forded in this upper section, but the algae-covered stones are very slippery.

WHITESTONE RIVER

☐ Location

Rises in the Livingstone Mountains west of Mavora Lakes and flows generally south to join the lower reaches of the Mararoa River in the Mt York area.

☐ Access

LOWER REACHES: From the Hillside–Manapouri road.

MIDDLE REACHES: From SH 94.

UPPER REACHES: Through private farmland off Kakapo Road, and the branch road to Mt Prospect that crosses the river.

☐ Season and restrictions

Below Prospect Bridge on Kakapo Road, 1 October–30 April. Above this bridge, 1 November–30 April. Bag limit is two trout.

This small freestone stream draining the Snowdon State Forest is a spawning stream and fishes best early in the season. By mid December most rainbows have drifted back downstream from the upper reaches. However, it does hold resident browns in the stable, deeper runs and pools. In long, hot summers, the river just upstream from the SH 94 bridge tends to dry and flow beneath the shingle. The majority of spawning fish are rainbows but some good-sized browns are also present. Most fish can be spotted and stalked as the river normally runs very clear. It is easy to wade and cross. Recent floods have had an adverse effect on this river.

MARAROA RIVER

Location

Rises near the Mararoa Saddle, flows south between the Livingstone and Thomson mountains and enters the north end of North Mavora Lake. Drains this lake and enters South Mavora Lake 4 km to the south. Emerges from South Mavora Lake and continues in a southerly direction for over 40 km before joining the Whitestone River in the Mt York area. After flowing through a gorge, the river joins the Waiau River 6.5 km south of Lake Manapouri, just above the Mararoa Weir.

Season and restrictions

1 October–30 April. The bag limit below Key Bridge on SH 94 is four trout, and two trout only above this bridge. It is illegal to fish from a boat or any other flotation device. Bait fishing is permitted below Key Bridge. For descriptive and geographical reasons, the river is divided into three sections.

Upper reaches (headwaters to South Mavora Lake)

Access

By boat to the top of North Mavora Lake and walking up the river.

By 4WD vehicle along the eastern side of North Mavora Lake. The track can be very rough and boggy in the first section and difficult if the lake is high.

By tramping to the headwaters over Mararoa Saddle from the Greenstone Valley. There are two DoC huts for basic accommodation: the first lies on the eastern lakeshore 1 km from the head of North Mavora Lake, and the second is 6 km upstream from the head of the lake.

The Upper Mararoa River drains small tarns in the headwaters and flows down a long, exposed tussock valley. It flows over a gravel bed and is small and easily crossed in this section. In the stretch upstream from the lake, there are browns and rainbows averaging 1.4 kg that are easy to spot on a sunny day. They can be carefully stalked and will take a wide variety of dry flies and nymphs. The Windon Burn, entering from the west, also holds a few good fish in its lower reaches early in the season. If you are prepared to walk up the valley over lumpy tussock there are some good-sized browns up to 3.5 kg, but these are much more difficult to deceive. Anglers arriving by boat to fish the river should realise that the 4WD track reaches the river about 1 km upstream from the lake. The nor'wester can ruin upstream fishing. It is a very long walk to the tarns in the headwaters but there can be fishing all the way. At times, the tarns also carry fish.

Between the lakes, the river is deep, clear and quite swift. There are very few fish.

Middle reaches (South Mavora Lake to SH 94)

☐ Access

SH 94 crosses the river just west of The Key. The Te Anau–Mavora Lakes road leaves SH 94 at Burwood Station and follows up the true left bank to the Mavora lakes. There is an access from the Mavora Station bridge and 'Angler Access' signs all along the Te Anau–Mavora Lakes road. The Centre Hill–Mavora Lakes road joins the Te Anau–Mavora Lakes road at the apex of a triangle.

At the southern end of South Mavora Lake, the medium-sized river flows through an inaccessible, rocky, bush-covered gorge and emerges 2 km upstream from the Kiwi Burn swingbridge. Tussock and patches of beech line the banks until the river leaves the bush and flows through pastoral land. As the river drains a stable lake it remains clear and fishable after rain, apart from exceptionally heavy downpours. Generally it fishes best in low-water summer conditions. Some fish can be seen along edges of runs and in pools, but many will be missed in the deeper, faster sections. The river is difficult to cross in the Kiwi Burn area but, as the valley widens and flattens out downstream in the pastoral section, the river braids and fording becomes possible at the tail of most pools. There are good stocks of fish (25 large fish per km) in the 1–3 kg range. Above the Kiwi Burn, 70 percent of fish are rainbow; below the Wood Burn, 70 percent are browns. The Kiwi Burn section is relatively sheltered in a nor'wester. Severe flooding in 1999 and 2002 seriously affected the river.

Lower reaches (SH 94 to Mararoa Weir)

☐ Access

By walking downstream from SH 94, or walking south through private farmland in the region of the Wilderness. There is a marked 'Angler Access' off SH 94 just east of the Wilderness.

About 1.5 km on the Manapouri side of the Hillside–Manapouri road bridge over the Whitestone River, there is a track on the left that leads downstream to the Whitestone confluence, Flaxy Creek and the top end of a gorge.

Weir Road from Manapouri crosses the river below a gorge and near the weir.

Above Weir Road bridge the river flows through a gorge, which can be negotiated by active anglers in low-water conditions only. Some of the crossings can be tricky. There are some deep, stable pools which a few local anglers fish successfully with live bait. Trout are hard to spot in this section but there is some good water for upstream nymph and dry-fly fishing in summer. Above this gorge the river braids and flows quite swiftly, with willows, broom and gorse obstructing casting on some sections. However, you are unlikely to meet other anglers on this section of river and there are some good-sized trout present in the more stable water.

A wide selection of flies will take fish on this river. Early in the season when the water is high, the swifter sections can be fished with two well weighted nymphs and an indicator. Later in summer, attractor-type dry flies provide good sport. Even well sunk Woolly Buggers fished across and downstream can bring results.

MAVORA LAKES

☐ Location

Between the Livingstone and Thomson mountains, south and west of Lake Wakatipu.

☐ Access

From SH 94 take the branch roads to Mavora Lakes from either Centre Hill or Burwood Station. These roads join and follow up the Mararoa River to the lakes. There is a basic camping area at North Mavora, but beware of sandflies.

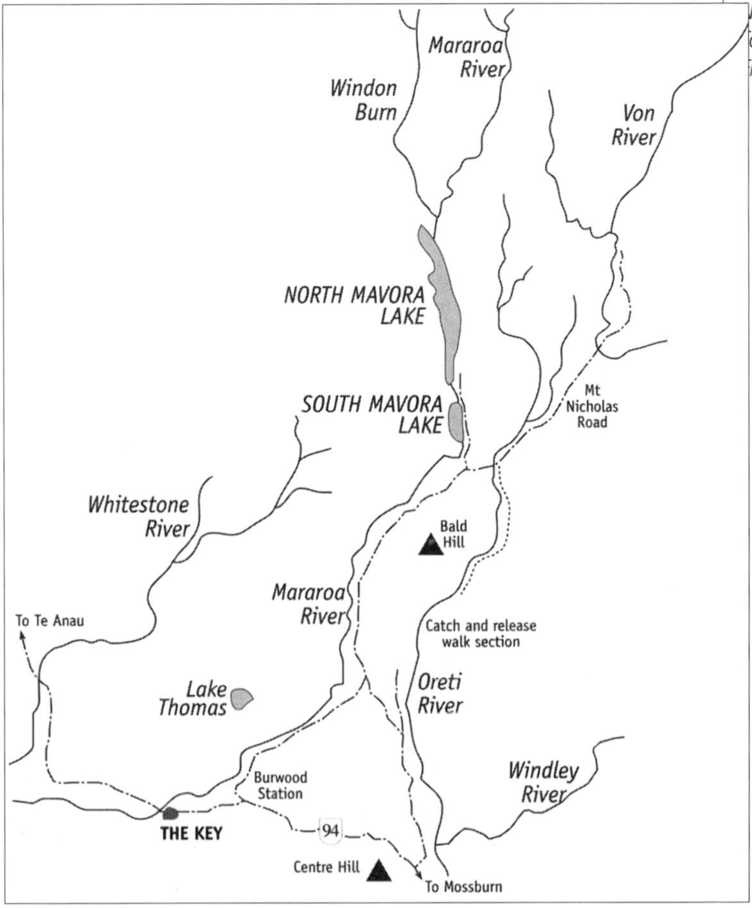

Mavora Lakes

☐ Season and restrictions

Open all year. Bag limit is four trout. Artificial bait and fly only.

☐ Boat launching

Small boats can be launched from the beach with a 4WD vehicle.

These are very scenic high-country lakes. North Mavora is 9.5 km long and apart from beech bush at the southern end it is surrounded by tussock and matagouri-covered mountains. The eastern shore can be readily accessed and there is a rough 4WD track to the head of the lake. The western shore requires a boat for access as the outlet is deep and swift. Both brown and rainbow trout in the 1.32 kg range can be stalked and ambushed around the lake edges with dry flies and nymphs. Many trout are caught from boats either trolling or harling a fly.

South Mavora Lake is much smaller (2.5 km long) and is more sheltered because it is surrounded by beech bush. Flycasting is more difficult but, at the open northern end of the lake where the river enters, there is good fly fishing for cruising trout. The sandflies can be fierce!

ORETI RIVER

☐ Location

Rises in the Thomson Mountains east of North Mavora Lake and flows south for over 130 km before entering the New River estuary just west of Invercargill.

☐ Season and restrictions

Open all year below the Invercargill–Riverton highway bridge (SH 99). Elsewhere, 1 October–30 April. From the headwaters to the downstream limit of the 'walk-only' zone, only one fish less than 40 cm can be taken. Downstream of the 'walk-only' zone to Rocky Point, the limit is two trout; and from Rocky Point to the sea, four trout.

Bait fishing is permitted only downstream of Rocky Point.

For descriptive purposes, the parts of this magnificent river that we consider worth fishing are divided into three sections. The lower reaches below Dipton, although they hold trout, are not considered prime fly-fishing waters, but trout can be taken on lures and spinners.

Headwaters ('walk-only' zone)

☐ Access

Take the Centre Hill–Mavora Lakes road off SH 94 and the short gravel Oreti Road to a carpark and locked gate. It is approximately a 16 km walk upstream to the upper Oreti bridge.

Alternatively, walk downstream from the upper Oreti bridge on the Mt Nicholas Road. Camping is not permitted.

This section of river is very exposed to nor'westerly winds and is best fished in a light southerly and bright sun. The valley is wide and flat and there is little background shadow to reduce the glare on the water for spotting fish. Trout are very difficult to spot in overcast conditions and many will be spooked. There is a good stock of browns averaging over 2 kg, and the occasional trophy fish is possible. The river flats and surrounding hills are tussock-covered with patches of beech bush. Crossings are easy on the stony riverbed and there are few trees to hinder casting. Early in the season, careful stalking and accurate casting with weighted nymphs accounts for most fish hooked. In December and January, mayfly and green beetle imitations are worth trying; and in February, large cicada, hopper and attractor-type flies can provide great sport.

Only a few fish inhabit the river upstream from the upper Oreti bridge. There is a farm track to walk back along after fishing. Angling pressure can be intense on this section of river. If someone has already parked at the gate, find another stretch of river to fish.

Upper reaches (below 'walk-only' zone to Rocky Point)

☐ Access

There are marked 'Angler Access' tracks off the Centre Hill–Mavora Lakes road. Further downstream below the Windley confluence there is an 'Angler Access' sign off SH 94 just west of Rocky Point. SH 94 runs close by the river at Rocky Point.

This section of river also holds some large browns, especially in the deeper runs and pools above the Windley River confluence. Below the confluence, the river spreads out over a wide shingly riverbed and in long, hot summers some fish will drop back downstream to deeper, more permanent water. Early in the season this section of river is well worth exploring but it is best on sunny days, when spotting and casting are easier. The riverbed is flat, without hills and scrub to reduce glare on the water. More walking is required between fish on this section of river.

Middle reaches (Rocky Point to Dipton)

☐ **Access**

From SH 94 between Rocky Point and Lumsden. From the Mossburn–Dipton road and SH 6. There are marked 'Angler Access' tracks off both these roads.

The river is unstable in this stretch and braids out on some sections. The valley is wide, shingly and flat and spotting trout is very difficult. Deeper runs and pools, especially those with one permanent bank, will usually hold fish and, although stocks may be higher than in the upper reaches, they tend to be smaller – on average, around 1 kg. Likely-looking stretches should be explored with dry flies, nymphs or even soft-hackle wet flies fished across and down. This last technique is most useful in strong downstream winds.

APPENDIX

New Zealand Professional Fishing Guides Association members

NORTH ISLAND

Eastern region

Frank and Antony
  Murphy's Lodge, PO Box 16, Motu
  ph (06) 863-5822
  fax (06) 863-5844

David Dods
  PO Box 38, Patutahi, Gisborne
  ph (06) 862-7850

Simon Hustler
  PO Box 2, Gisborne
  ph (06) 862-4809
  fax (06) 862-4877

Rick Pollock
  62 Arawa Rd, Whakatane
  ph (07) 308-5442
  fax (07) 307-1242

Grant Petherick
  805 Fitzroy Ave, Hastings
  ph 025 863-924
  fax (06) 876-7467

Robbie Greenslade
  32 Rawiri St, Gisborne
  ph (06) 867-1214
  fax (06) 863-1263

John Renolds
  Ruatahunga, RD1, Tolaga Bay
  ph (06) 862-6741
  fax (06) 862-6781

Morris Hill
  27 Tainui Drive, Havelock North
  ph (06) 877-7642
  fax (06) 877-7542

Rotorua district

Bryan Coleman
  32 Kiwi St, Rotorua
  ph (07) 348-7766
  fax (07) 347-9852

Clark Gregor
  33 Haumoana St, Rotorua
  ph (07) 347-1123
  fax (07) 347-1732

Hajime Kaneko
  44 Rotokawa Rd, RD4, Rotorua
  ph (07) 348-1047
  fax (07) 348-1049

Michael Cassidy
  c/o Murupara Motel, Box 97, Murupara

Toshiya Babe (TB Enterprise)
  93 Meadowbank Rd, Auckland,
  fax (09) 528-2990

Greg Tuuta
  PDC State Highway 30
  Lake Rotoiti, Rotorua
  ph (07) 362-7794
  fax (07) 362-7792

Taupo/Turangi district

B.H. Wrathall
  79 Namotu Rd, Taupo
  ph (07) 348-9844

Peter Church Fishing Guides
  13 Rangiamohia Rd, Turangi
  ph (07) 386-8621

Simon Dickie
  PO Box 682, Taupo
  ph (07) 378-9680

Ken Drummond
  PO Box 186, Turangi

Tony Hayes
PO Box 278 Turangi
ph (07) 386-7946
fax (07) 386-8860
Chris Jolly
PO Box 1020, Taupo
ph (07) 378-0623
Tim McCarthy
PO Box 89, Turangi
ph (07) 386-8207
Graham Pyatt, 'Dyden'
Old Mill Lane, Grace Rd, RD2, Turangi
ph (07) 386-6032
Paddy Clark
1246 Poihipi Road, RD1, Taupo
fax (07) 378-2331
Graham Dean
c/o The Store, Te Rangiita, Turangi
ph (07) 386-0726
fax (07) 386-0497
Mike Stent
44 Lakewood Drive, Taupo
ph/fax (07) 378-4449
Graham Whyman
c/o Sporting Life, Turangi
Carol Harwood
PO Box 290, Turangi
ph/fax (07) 386-7929
Ian Ruthven
PO Box 1725, Taupo
ph/fax (07) 378-4514
Alan Simmons
48 Gosling St, Turangi
ph/fax (07) 386-7576
Kerry Simpson
Ika Lodge 155 Tuapahi Rd, Turangi
ph/fax (07) 386-7341
Stephen Yerex
PO Box 1514, Taupo
ph/fax (07) 377-3202
Michael Rowntree
Turangi
ph/fax (07) 386-7953
Ross Hamilton
Turangi
ph (07) 386-6393
fax (07) 386-0660
Peter Fordham
Taupo
phone (07) 378-8454
fax (07) 378-8494
Ron Burgin
PO Box 1488, Taupo
ph/fax (07) 378-3126
Grant Bayley
88 Taupo Rd, Taupo
ph (07) 377-605
fax (07) 377-6136
Andrew Jenkins
28 Tahawai St, Turangi
ph/fax (07) 386-0840
Ian Jenkins
28 Tahawai St, Turangi
ph/fax (07) 386-0840
Ken Duncan
11 Ward Pl, Taupo
fax (07) 377-0058

Wellington district

David Webb
143 Oxford St, Ashurst
ph (06) 326-8423

SOUTH ISLAND

Alexandra district

Lloyd Knowles
Earnscleugh, No 1 RD, Alexandra
ph (03) 449-212

Canterbury district

John Bufton
2 Moana Square, Christchurch
ph/fax (03) 308-5461
Kevin Frazier
104 Elizabeth St, Ashburton
ph (03) 308-5963
fax (03) 308-1353

Shane Johnston
20 Powell Cres, Avonhead, Christchurch
ph (03) 358-6223

Tony Allan
65 Ocean View Tce, Christchurch
ph (03) 326-5611
fax (03) 384-1477

Bill Allison
211 West Belt, Rangiora
ph/fax (03) 313-8007

Richard Halkett
Morris Lane, Pleasant Point

Basil Ivey
Cairn Hollow, RD5, Ashburton
ph (03) 303-6078

Ross Marks
12 Road Rd, Fendalton, Christchurch
ph (03) 348-2414
fax (03) 379-0988

Brian Minty
17 Awamoa Rd, Oamaru
ph (03) 434-7105

Eric Prattley
Wallingford Rd, Temuka
ph (03) 615-9386

Harvey Taylor
34 Greenhurst St, Christchurch
ph (03) 348-1971

Kevin Taylor
Sycamore Ave, 12th Barrhil
ph/fax (03) 302-1841

Geoff Scott
14th Rakaia
phone (03) 302-7444

Steve Gerard
13 Cameron St, Methven
ph (03) 302-8448
fax (03) 302-8441

Robert Vaile
Arthur's Pass, Canterbury
ph (03) 318-9215

Chappie Chapman
Canterbury
ph/fax (03) 359-5440
mobile 025 393 490

Mark Eastmond
157 Lower Flat Rd, Waiau, North Canterbury
fax (03) 315-6173

Kevin Payne
20 Murray St, Temuka
ph (03) 615-6101

Barry Sinclair
11 Lismore St, Oamaru
ph/fax (03) 437-1750

Cromwell district

Dick Marquand
PO Box 32, Cromwell
ph/fax (03) 445-1745
mobile 025 344 258

Kenneth McGraw
Wakefield East, RD3, Cromwell
ph/fax (03) 445-0516

Gore district

John Hannabus
23 Milton St, Gore
ph (03) 208-4922
fax (03) 208-9252

Bryan Burgess
6 Mitre St, Gore
ph (03) 208-0801
fax (03) 208-7849

David Murray-Orr
Box 111, Gore

Daniel Agar
Box 47, Mataura
ph (03) 442-4373
mobile 025 223 2007

Mackenzie Country, Omarama, Twizel

Steven Carey
'Aoraki Lodge', Twizel
ph (03) 435-0300
fax (03) 435-0305

Frank Schlosser
PO Box 124, Omarama
ph/fax (03) 680-6797

Tony Murphy
PO Box 1211, Queenstown
phone (03) 442-9656
fax (03) 442-8565
Max Irons
9 Black Peak Rd, Omarama
ph (03) 438-9468
Allan Campbell
Glenburn Park
fax (03) 438-9624
Grant Brown
36 Murray Pl, Lake Tekapo
fax (03) 680-6516

Nelson/Marlborough/ West Coast

Timothy Barnett, 'Windhawk',
Omaka Valley, RD2
ph (03) 578-0947
fax (03) 572-9560
John Boyles
RD1, Blackball, Greymouth
ph (03) 732-3531
Graeme Brunwin
Motupiko RD, Nelson
ph (03) 522-4052
John Brunwin
97 Murphy St, Nelson
ph (03) 548-9145
fax (03) 548-9146
Peter Carty
Chalgrave St, Murchison
ph (03) 523-9525
Boris Cech, Kehu Guiding
RD2 Rotoiti, Nelson
ph/fax (03) 521-1840
Tony Entwistle
5 Mason Pl, Richmond, Nelson
ph (03) 544-4565
Peter Flintoft
18 Hampden St, Murchison
ph (03) 523-9315
Ron McKay
31 Hotham St, Murchison 7191
ph (03) 523-9533
Graeme Marshall
Ngatimoti RD1, Motueka
ph (03) 526-8800
Zane Mirfin
Baxter St PDC, St Arnaud 7150
ph (03) 521-1017
Lindsay White
PO Box 68, Murchison
ph/fax (03) 523-9114
David Heine
111 Shakespeare St, Greymouth
ph/fax (03) 768-6415
Peter Warren
Pigeon Valley Lodge, 2 RD, Wakefield, Nelson
Gregory Chisnall
Nelson
ph (03) 542-3525
fax (03) 542-3891
Murray Scott
174 Westbrook St, Nelson
ph (03) 548-7826
Brent Beadle
Moana Hotel, Moana
William Woollcombe
Ashbury RD1, Blenheim
mobile 025 446 198
fax (03) 578-9360
Mark Meumann
Waiwhero Road, RD1, Motueka
ph (03) 526-8086
Brian Hoy
Postal Delivery Centre, Paroa, Greymouth
ph/fax (03) 762-6010
Silvio Edmund
9 Larsen St, Cape Foulwind, RD2, Westport
ph/fax (03) 789-5686
Russell Frost
PO Box 30, Murchison
ph/fax (03) 523-9371
Bryan Wilson
PO Box 14, Reefton
mobile 025 245 8163

Michael Buchanan
15 Grey St, Murchison
ph/fax (03) 523-9196

Northern Southland

Len Prentice
Athol Post Office
fax (03) 248 8890

Otago

Bryan Minty
17 Awamoa Rd, Oamaru
fax (03) 434-7103

Barry Sinclair
11 Lismore St, Oamaru
ph/fax (03) 437-1750

Daryl Whiston
11 Lismore St Oamaru
ph/fax (03) 437-1750

Graeme Warren
104 Gordon St, Kurow
ph/fax (03) 436-0510
mobile 025 242 8623

Gavin Pegley
7 Henderson St, Mornington, Dunedin
ph/fax (03) 453-6679

Selwyn Shanks
PO Box 1293, Dunedin
ph (03) 477-3266
mobile 025 347 459

Queenstown district

Steve Couper
PO Box 149, Wakatipu
ph/fax (03) 442-3589

Dick Fraser
PO Box 145, Queenstown
ph/fax (03) 442-6069

Harvey Maguire
334 Littles Rd, Queenstown 9197
fax (03) 442-9088

Jeff Jones
PO Box 624, Queenstown
ph (03) 442-6570
fax (03) 441-8808

Ron Stewart
c/o Postal Centre, Glenorchy
ph/fax (03) 442-9966

Geoff McDonald, PO Box 443, Queenstown
ph/fax (03) 442-8706

George Moore
Unit 2/34 Dublin St, Queenstown
ph (03) 442-5230
fax (03) 442-5326

Nick Clark
Closeburn, Queenstown
ph (03) 442-9401
fax (03) 442-9404

Grant Alley
Frankton, Queenstown
ph/fax (03) 442-9208

Ken Cochrane
PO Box 527, Queenstown
ph/fax (03) 442-9413

Trevor Cruickshank
9b York St, Queenstown
ph (03) 442-4462

Ed Halson
5 Arthurs Track, Queenstown
ph (03) 442-5236

Southland

Alan Wilson
411 Herbert St, Invercargill
ph/fax (03) 217-3687

Daryl Pascall
141 Patterson St, Invercargill
ph (03) 218-7084

Dennis Collins
9 Baird St, Invercargill
ph/fax (03) 217-2890
mobile 021 136 3367

Te Anau district

Murray Knowles
PO Box 84, Te Anau
ph (03) 249-7565
fax (03) 249-7564

Ron Todd
PO Box 204, Te Anau
ph/fax (03) 249-8499

Dean Bell
PO Box 198, Te Anau
ph (03) 249-7847
fax (03) 217-3755

Mike Molineux
Box 31, Manapouri
ph (03) 249-8070
fax (03) 249-8470

Michael Bednar
40 Cathedral Dr, Manapouri
ph/fax (03) 249-6996

Wanaka district

Arthur Gray
39 Matai St, Wanaka
ph/fax (03) 443-7279

Gerald Telford
PO Box 312, Wanaka
ph/fax (03) 443-9257

Richard Grimmett
37 Hunter Cres, Wanaka
ph (03) 443-7748

Ian Cole
43 Russell St, Wanaka
ph/fax (03) 443-7870

Ken Mitchell
7 Ardmore St, Wanaka
ph (03) 443-7950
fax (03) 443-9031

Dan Orbell
Larchwood Lodge, Dublin Bay, Wanaka
ph (03) 443-7914

GLOSSARY

4WD four-wheel-drive vehicle; in this book, refers to a vehicle specifically designed for off-road use, with suitable tyres and good ground clearance

angler access legal access for anglers, arranged by local Fish and Game Councils after negotiation with the landowner

bach (pronounced 'batch') term used in northern and central areas for a holiday house or cottage (see also 'crib')

crib term used in southern areas for a holiday house or cottage (see also 'bach')

dairy small grocery store, usually open extended hours

fly fishing in New Zealand, legally defined by the casting weight being in the line itself; it therefore excludes the use of a fly attached to monofilament nylon on a spinning outfit, or use of a discrete weight such as a lead sinker to assist casting

fresh (also 'freshet') a rush or sudden flood of water in a creek or river

fresh run a new run or group of fish running or moving up a river or stream

harling trolling a fly behind a boat, usually with a fly rod

koura freshwater crayfish

kowhai medium-sized tree with yellow flowers, common on riverbanks

lure in New Zealand, a larger type of wet fly (typically size 8 or bigger) that usually imitates a small fish or crayfish

manuka native shrub of myrtle family, with small white or pink flowers, also known as teatree

matagouri prickly native shrub with small yellow flowers, especially common in South Island high country; ranks alongside gorse as the most problematic plant on the backcast

National Water Conservation Orders statutes incorporated in the Resource Management Act

papa mudstone

paper road track that has been surveyed as a road, but no road has been built; farm track

scrub dense low bushes; a common hindrance when casting or walking

smelt a very small, usually silvery, freshwater fish

smelting fish trout which are chasing smelt that congregate in the shallows for spawning

sports fish includes brown trout, rainbow trout, American brook trout or char, lake trout or char, Atlantic salmon, quinnat or chinook salmon, sockeye salmon, perch, tench and rudd, and any hybrid of these mentioned species

streamer fly see 'lure'

toetoe native grass, similar to pampas grass – grows to 2 m, with feather duster-like plumes; often overhangs riverbanks and impedes casting but provides good shelter for fish

tramping travelling on foot with a backpack containing equipment and provisions for overnight or longer

true left bank *looking downstream* the bank that is on the left

true right bank *looking downstream* the bank that is on the right

wapiti large elk, also called American elk

ABOUT the authors

John Kent is a retired medical practitioner with over 50 years' trout fishing experience in both the North and South Island. He has a lifelong enthusiasm for New Zealand's back country and is the author of three other books, including the best-selling *North Island Trout Fishing Guide* and *South Island Trout Fishing Guide* (both published by Reed Publishing). John has given presentations on trout fishing in New Zealand to the International Federation of Fly Fishers (FFF) conclaves in the United States, and was awarded the inaugural Fish and Game Gold Medal for his campaign against 'dirty dairying'.

Patti Magnano Madsen first came to New Zealand 15 years ago for one month of fishing and literally stayed, fishing being the lure. She is a FFF-certified flycasting instructor and has taught with Mel Krieger in the United States, Canada and Argentina, as well as fly-tying classes at the FFF conclaves in Montana, Oregon, Idaho and Michigan. When not fishing – which is not often – she can be found biking, sailing and tying flies. Patti and John live eight months of every year in Christchurch and four in Seattle.

INDEX